HOW TO SEW
Leather, Suede, Fur

HOW TO SEW
Leather, Suede, Fur

REVISED EDITION

PHYLLIS W. SCHWEBKE

MARGARET B. KROHN

COLLIER BOOKS
A Division of Macmillan Publishing Co., Inc.
NEW YORK

COLLIER MACMILLAN PUBLISHERS
LONDON

The authors and publishers wish to thank the following for the photographs used in this book:

Leathers and Suedes: Courtesy of Begador/Denise Originals, Inc.

Leather Maxi (p. 1): Courtesy of McCall's Step-by-Step Catalogue, Pattern #2279.

Fur Vest (p. 69): Courtesy of Vogue Pattern Book International, Pattern #7515.

Furs: On pp. 71, 73 (Figures 1 and 2), and 137, courtesy of David G. Kaplan Fine Furs; on p. 73 (cloche), courtesy of Parloné Furs.

Library of Congress Catalog Card Number: 76-123531

MACMILLAN PUBLISHING CO., INC.
866 THIRD AVENUE, NEW YORK, N.Y. 10022
COLLIER-MACMILLAN CANADA LTD.

FIRST COLLIER BOOKS EDITION 1974

THIRD PRINTING 1975

Printed in the United States of America

FOREWORD

This book has been written to assist the home sewer and student in the fashioning of garments from leather, suede, and fur. It may be used not only at home, but in the adult education, college, or high school classroom.

It is assumed that the person who creates garments and accessories from leather, suede, and fur has some knowledge and skill in the fundamentals of sewing. In this book, we have attempted to present, briefly and concisely, the basic techniques of sewing with leather, suede, and fur. This has been done in a step-by-step format with numerous illustrations so that the person who uses this book will have as much information and help as she needs to make fine garments and accessories.

The authors wish to express their appreciation to their former students in their classes during the years the materials were tested. They are grateful to Mrs. Willard L. Fuller for the inspiring fashion sketches. Mrs. Krohn desires to thank her husband, Dr. Armin F. Krohn, and her children, Timothy, Jennifer, and Priscilla; and, Mrs. Schwebke, her husband, Prof. Howard Schwebke, her sons, John and James, and her American Field Service son, Risto Savilahti, for their loyal support and encouragement during this endeavor.

The authors dedicate this book to those who desire to create fashionable garments from leather, suede, and fur.

CONTENTS

DRAWING KEY

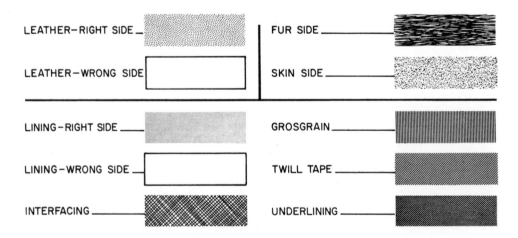

LEATHER—RIGHT SIDE

LEATHER—WRONG SIDE

LINING—RIGHT SIDE

LINING—WRONG SIDE

INTERFACING

FUR SIDE

SKIN SIDE

GROSGRAIN

TWILL TAPE

UNDERLINING

The various drawings indicate the characteristics of the materials to be used. By comparing the shadings in the drawings throughout the book with this key, you will be able to select the appropriate material for the job.

LEATHER
AND
SUEDE

McCall's Pattern # 2279

1

LEATHER—
THEN AND
NOW

HISTORY OF LEATHER
AND SUEDE

Leather has played an important role in the development of civilization. From prehistoric times man has used the skins of animals to satisfy his basic needs. He has used hides to make clothing, shelter, carpets, and even decorative attire. To the Egyptian lady, a fur piece was as highly prized as her jewelry. From leather, man made footwear, belts, clothing, containers for liquids, boats, and even armor. The principal protective armor of the Roman soldier was a heavy leather shirt.

In recorded history, pieces of leather dating from 1300 B.C. have been found in Egypt. Primitive societies in Europe, Asia, and North America all developed the technique of turning skins into leather goods independently of one another. The Greeks were using leather garments in the age of the Homeric heroes (about 1200 B.C.), and the use of leather later spread throughout the Roman Empire. During the Middle Ages, the Chinese knew the art of making leather. The Indians of North America also had developed great skills in leatherwork before the coming of the white man.

At some time, by accident or by trial and error, man discovered methods of preserving and softening leather by treating animal skins with such things as smoke, grease, and bark extracts. The art of tanning leather using the bark of trees probably originated among the Hebrews. In primitive societies, the art was a closely guarded secret passed down from father to son. As civilization developed in Europe, tanners and leatherworkers united in the trade guilds of the Middle Ages, as did the craftsmen in other fields. Royal charters or licenses were issued permitting people to practice leather tanning. In 1620 Experience Miller brought the knowledge of tanning to the early English colonies in America. In the nineteenth century, vegetable tanning, i.e., tanning using extracts from the bark of certain kinds of trees, was supplemented by chrome tanning. This process uses chemicals and today accounts for about ninety percent of all tanning done in the United States except for the leather used in the soles of shoes and tooling leathers.

In recent years, about 75 million hides have been used in the leather industry annually. Leather goods contribute about 1.7 billion dollars to our gross national product every year. Most of the leather (about eighty-five percent) is used in the manufacture of shoes.

PREPARATION OF LEATHER AND SUEDE

Leather and suede are made from the hides of domestic and wild animals. The process by which these hides and skins are transformed into supple, pliable leathers is called tanning. The two principal methods of tanning are vegetable tanning and chrome tanning.

Vegetable tanning uses the extracts from tree bark. Since the finished leather produced by this process absorbs moisture, this leather is used when tooling is required. Also, shoe soles, luggage, upholstery, and harnesses are made from vegetable-tanned leather. However, vegetable tanning is a long and expensive process and for many leather products, it has been replaced by chrome tanning. It is a much faster and less expensive method than vegetable tanning. Hence, it is used for almost all the leather to be used in making shoe uppers, gloves, and garments. Chrome tanning makes leather resistant to water, though not waterproof since leather is porous. However, the fibers of the leather are tightened and the tensile strength is increased.

Sometimes a combination of these two methods is used and this is referred to as "retanning" or "combination tanning."

In brief, the processes involved in the making of leather and suede are:

Curing and Cleaning.
1. The hide is salted for ten to fifteen days.
2. The hair is removed with a lime solution and then a dehairing machine.
3. Flesh is removed by a machine.
4. Scudding or scraping the skin by hand removes any remaining hair or flesh.

Tanning.
1. Hides are placed on racks and soaked in the tanning solution. In vegetable tanning they are moved to stronger vats from day to day.
2. The tanning solution is washed out.

Shaving.
If the leather is uneven in thickness, it is shaved in thick spots.

Drying.

Toggling, Staking, or Brushing.
1. In toggling, the leather is stretched to remove excess elasticity.
2. In staking, the leather, which has formed an exterior coat during the tanning process, is washed over metal stakes to break the crust and make the leather pliable.
3. In brushing, the leather is cleaned and made soft and pliable by working it with brushes.

Sorting.
The leather is graded according to specific characteristics of quality.

Coloring and Finishing.
1. Natural leather is plated (ironed).
2. Smaller hides are dyed in tumblers, toggled, and dried.
3. Color is sprayed on larger hides.

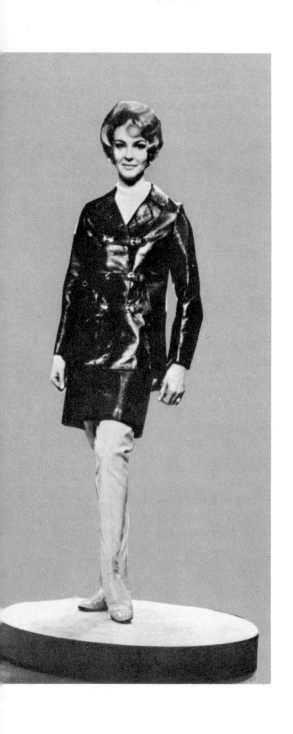

4 *LEATHER AND SUEDE*

4. An embossed design simulating the skin of another animal may be plated or ironed on some skins to give them a more expensive appearance.
5. In the Levant Process, the leather is crushed to give it the appearance of fine Levant morocco which has large, irregular grain patterns.
6. In glazing, the leather is polished on a glass cylinder to produce a high-gloss finish.

Measuring.
1. Machines measure the surface area of the leather, even allowing for the holes.
2. Gauges are used to measure the thickness of the leather.

Grading.
1. Grading is done by the human eye and hand.
2. See "How do you order leather?" on p. 9.

PREPARING DEER, ELK, AND MOOSE HIDES FOR TANNING

1. Skin the animal carefully to avoid cuts and breaks.

2. Spread the rawhide flat with the flesh side up as soon as the skin is removed and remove any remnants of tallow or flesh. If left on, this material heats the hide and results in a poor quality leather.
3. Sprinkle water softener or livestock salt liberally over the entire flesh side.
4. Allow the hide to remain flat for at least twenty-four hours before shipping.
5. Roll the hide onto a cylinder leaving the salt inside. Do not fold, stretch, or lay the hide flat before tanning.
6. Prepare the hide for shipping to the tannery:
   a) Tie the hide securely with twine.
   b) Put it in a burlap bag or a sturdy paper carton.
   c) Ship it express, prepaid, and properly tagged.
7. Chart the hide for size from various dressed weights of deer:

Deer 90 to 125 lb.—Small
Deer 125 to 150 lb.—Medium small
Deer 155 to 180 lb.—Medium large
Deer 180 to 200 lb.—Large
Deer over 200 lb.—Extra large

2

SELECTING
LEATHER
FOR
CLOTHING

WHY LEATHER AND SUEDE GARMENTS?

Leather has been called "nature's gift to man." Clothes made of leather and suede allow ventilation, absorption, and evaporation of moisture. In other words, it "breathes." The millions of tiny air spaces among the fibers provide insulation and ventilation for warmth in the winter and comfort in the summer. It is ideal for high fashion costumes or sportswear. In Italy, Germany, England, and the Scandinavian countries, as well as in America, leather and suede are gaining in importance as a material for apparel. Leather is practically indestructible, easily cleaned, comfortable to wear, and easy to work on, since it drapes well and is sewn like fabric. Leather is used for coats, jackets, suits, slacks, dresses (floor length or short), jumpers and vests, various trims, and as panels let into skirts and sweaters. Suede has taken the top selling spot in many parts of the country, supplanting leathers and kidskins.

WHAT KINDS OF LEATHERS ARE USED FOR GARMENTS?

A soft leather is desirable for making garments. There are many leathers tanned expressly for garments such as goatskin, calfskin, buckskin, horsehide, cowhide, and some steerhides. The covering of smaller animals, such as calves, sheep, and goats, which weigh less than 15 pounds, is referred to as *skin*. A *hide* is taken from a larger animal of 25 pounds or more. *Kip* is the term used for sizes between 15 and 25 pounds. It is interesting to note that no animal produces both fur and leather.

Some leathers are used expressly for garments, but others have many other uses (Figure 1). Fashion garment leathers are usually suede and capeskin. Suedes are from the inside skin of young lambs. Smooth leathers from lambskin

Pigskin—gloves, saddles, luggage, undersoles, etc.

 Buckskin— gloves, uppers of shoes

 Cowhide—soles, and uppers for shoes, luggage, etc.

 Goatskin— women's shoes, suede, handbags

 Sheepskin— slippers, handbags, chamois, hat bands, et

 Calfskin—shoes, handbags, gloves, luggage, etc.

Figure 1

Figure 2

Suede coat with piped seam edges

are capeskin, cabretta, kidskin (not imported glove kidskin), and glacé leather. Most of the patina on "reptile" leather has been artificially applied.

A *garment suede* is a specially selected New Zealand lambskin with a silky nap and can be used for jackets, hats, and coats (Figure 2). The skins average 6 to 8 square feet in size and come in approximately twelve colors. Suede which is hand washable and commercially dry cleanable will soon be available.

Sheer suedes for skirts, dresses, jumpers and suits are available by various names as *Antelamb, Plainsman Sheer,* and *Sewsoft Sheer suede.* This leather is lightweight, soft and supple, and handles like fine fabric.

Capeskin is a smooth, full-grain, imported lambskin which is used for coats, jackets, matching hats, and bags. The skins average 6 to 9 square feet in size. A

shelter cape is available at one company in white only and is treated by spraying to resist soiling. It can be cleaned with a sponge and soap and water. *Princess garment lamb* is another brand name leather used for jackets, coats, skirts, and vests. It is available in pastels and many darker colors. *Garment Cabretta* is a popular smooth capeskin garment leather with a distinctive character. It is available in black, brown, tan, red, white, and beige. *Buck-Tanned Cowhide* is a fine cream color cowhide in 20 to 25 foot sides used for Indian garments. *Softan Garment Cowhide* is a cowhide ideal for jackets and coats. It is available in black, brown, beige, and white.

Glove Horse is a soft, supple, easy-to-handle horsehide for outdoor jackets and coats which one expects to give hard wear. This leather is available in cream and pearl in 15 to 20 foot sides.

Hair Calf is a skin with the hair remaining, as the name suggests. The grade of this skin is determined by the marking pattern and the lack of bald spots. In *Short-Hair Calf,* the hair of the animal is left its natural length. Short hair calfskins range from 4 to 6 square feet. Another type of hair calf is *Clipped Hair Calf;* it has been smoothly sheared. It is excellent for garments requiring short hair and large skins.

Cobra is a snakeskin with a definite, flat scale. The full skin averages about 4½ to 5 inches wide and 4½ to 5 feet long. It is dyed in many colors. Cobraskins are used for vests, belts, buttons, collars, and welt pockets. It is available in cording by the yard for edging garments and other trimming.

Deerskin (Figure 3) is a hide from deer averaging 7 to 12 square feet. It is available in black, gray, cork, oatmeal, natural, and white.

Shearling is sheepskin tanned with the wool on. The nap may vary in length from ¼ to ¾ inch. It is used for cold weather garments. Shearling comes in dark beige, pink, blue, and white with brown backs. The skins range from 6 to 10 square feet.

Peccary is pigskin which has a smooth finish with a grained effect since the bristles have been removed. It is soft, pliable, and durable. The skins are generally from 5 to 7½ square feet and are available in cork, oatmeal, white, black, and gray. *Pigtex* or *Pecca Pig* are trade names for lambskins embossed or marked to resemble natural pigskin. The skins average 5 to 7 square feet and come in brown, natural, black, green, cork, red, wine, gray, and oatmeal.

Kidskin is imported goatskin; it is a sturdy leather, very soft and pliable. It is often used in suede.

Antique leather refers to a mottled finish in a textured kidskin with a soft patina handle.

G.M.L. (genuine milled leather) is a yard goods with pulverized leather applied to a textile backing, dyed in leather tones and patterned. It is used for tailored clothes and evening gowns as well as for children's clothes. The surface may be refreshed with a sponge or cloth dipped in suds or cleaning fluid or it may be dry-cleaned.

HOW DO YOU ORDER LEATHER?

Small skins, such as goat, calf, or lamb (suedes), are usually sold in the whole skin. A calf usually runs from 9 to 15 square feet and sheep and goats from 5

Figure 3

Deerskin vest combined with wool

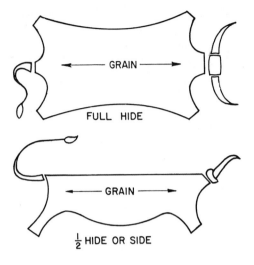

Figure 4

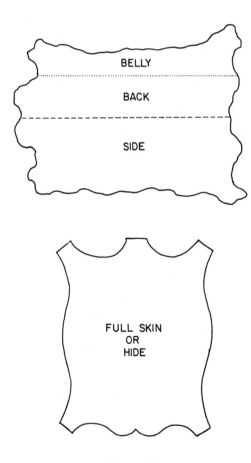

Figure 5

to 9 square feet. A *side* refers to one half a full skin (Figure 4). The lower part of a side is called the *belly*. The choice part of a side is the *back* which has less waste than the side and costs more because the belly was removed (Figure 5).

Because leather is not manufactured as is fabric, it is less uniform than other sewing materials. There are many factors which may cause a variation in the skin or hide of an animal such as the age, climatic conditions, the food and care given it, the season in which it was slaughtered, and the skill used in tanning.

Leather dealers use ounces to designate the relative thickness of leather. One-ounce leather weighs 1 ounce per square foot; 3-ounce leather weighs 3 ounces per square foot, and so on. One-ounce leather is approximately $\frac{1}{64}$ inch thick. Since the weight and thickness of one hide varies slightly, the markings may read $\frac{7}{8}$ ounce. Such a piece of leather would weigh between 7 and 8 ounces per square foot and be $\frac{7}{64}$ or $\frac{8}{64}$ inches in thickness. Figure 6 is a scale for determining the thickness of leather.

There are no exact standards or methods for grading leather since it is done by "sight and feel" developed through training and experience. Thus, a given grade may vary slightly from time to time. Leathers are graded 1, 2, 3, 4, and so forth, or A, B, C, D, DX. Since there is less leather produced in grade 1 or A, the price is higher. The grade does not affect the wearing quality, but it does affect the useable portion of the hide.

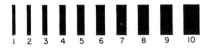

Figure 6

The higher numbered grades have more imperfections, holes, stains, and scratches.

Patterns usually call for material in terms of yards, while leather is sold by the foot. Since skins vary in size, it is wise to send a copy of your pattern in brown paper with the grainline marked to the leather supplier. A formula is used for the purpose of converting fabric yardage to leather footage. The conversion factor is 9 if the pattern calls for 36-inch fabric and 13 if the pattern suggests 54-inch fabric. Fifteen to twenty percent is added for loss in cutting.

Example:

Pattern calls for 2 yd. of 36-in. fabric—conversion factor 9	2 yd. ×9
	18
allow for loss— 15%	× .15
	2.7
add to 18	+ 18
	20.7 or 21 sq. ft.
Pattern calls for 2 yd. of 54-in. fabric—conversion factor 13	2 yd. × 13
	26
allow for loss:	× .15
large skins 15%	3.19
small skins 20%	+ 26
	29.9 or 30 sq. ft.

A common general guide for leather footage for garments is: 30 square feet for a short jacket, 55 to 60 square feet for a ¾ length coat and 72 square feet for a full-length coat.

The following is a guide for the approximate number of suede skins needed for garments:

ladies vest—2 skins
man's vest—2 skins; fabric back
overblouse—3 skins
short jacket with collar and sleeves—
    5 skins
A-line skirt—4 skins

For capeskin (Cabretta), the following number of skins is suggested:

vest—2 skins
jacket with sleeves—3 skins
slacks—2 skins

The approximate number of deer hides for jackets is:

Small hide   —4 to 5 per jacket
Medium small—3 to 4
Medium large—3
Large   —3
Extra large   —2 to 3
Vests require 1 large deer hide.
Sport coats require 4 medium deer
    hides.
Women's full-length coats require 6
    to 7 large deer hides.
Women's car coats require 4 large
    deer hides.

3

EQUIPMENT AND SUPPLIES

The equipment and supplies needed for sewing leather and suede are similar to those used for dressmaking with a few exceptions. A special triangular sewing machine needle and a hand sewing needle are essential to penetrate leather and suede with a clean cut. A leather supply company, dressmaker supplier, or the department store notion counter can supply these and other items.

EQUIPMENT

Awl. A sharply pointed instrument with a handle used to pierce holes in heavy leather prior to hand stitching (Figure 7).

Ball-point pen. Used for marking the leather on the wrong side and for alteration markings on the basic muslin pattern.

Beeswax. A cake of pure beeswax used to wax hand sewing thread to give it added strength, to keep it from tangling, and to slip it more easily through the leather (Figure 8).

Crayon, wax (often referred to as *tailor's chalk*). A wax crayon available in colors, used interchangeably with a ball-point pen for marking the skins on the underside (Figure 9). A *clay chalk* is used to mark lining materials.

Cutting tools.
> *Razor blade.* A single-edge razor blade used to cut heavier leathers and to skive seams to reduce bulk.
> *Furrier's knife.* A holder in which a razor blade is placed (Figure 10).
> *Shears.* A sharp pair of dressmaker's shears, 7½ to 8 inches long, used to cut out garments. It may be used at an angle to skive seams.

Glue. A good quality rubber cement or a leather cement available in a tube, ¼-pint jar, quart, or gallon container. It is used to flatten seams, darts, buttonhole pieces, and hems. A cement jar or can with a bristle brush attached is convenient to prevent evaporation and for easier application of the cement. A plastic-bulb ear syringe may also be used as an applicator.

NOTE: Genuine rubber cement remains flexible and will not crack (Figure 11). Other liquid adhesives suitable for leather or fabric are *Sobo* cement, *Barge* cement, and *Tehr-Greeze*.

Knife. A beveled-edge leather-skiving knife (Figure 12), X-acto knife (Figure 13), a safety beveler which uses razor blades,

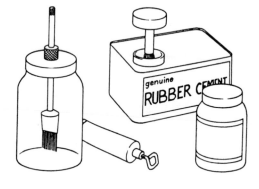

Figure 11

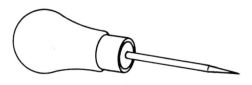

Figure 7

Figure 8

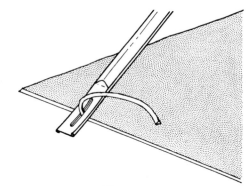

Figure 12

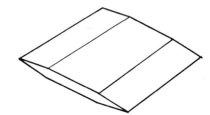

Figure 9

Figure 10

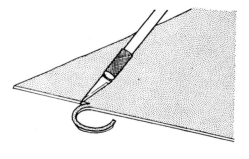

Figure 13

or a single-edge razor (Figure 14) used to skive the seams or detailed areas.

Mallet. A hammerlike tool made from water buffalo hide and used to tap seams and flatten other construction areas (Figure 15). A hickory mallet may also be used. A piece of scrap leather fastened with a rubber band may be placed over the head of the mallet or hammer. A croquet mallet may be used as a substitute.

Needles.

Glover needle. A three-cornered needle which penetrates the leather easily. Usually found in an assorted needle pack in a size 4. Sizes 5 to 6 are finer needles used for soft, lightweight skins (Figure 16).

Sewing machine needle (15 x 2). A wedge-point needle available in an assorted pack in sizes 11, 14, and 16. A size 11 needle is used for sheer suedes, kidskin, fine capeskin, and soft leathers. For medium-weight leathers, firm capeskin, and suede, use a size 14. The size 16 is best for heavier-weight capeskin, lined leathers, or stitching 3-ply or more together.

Sharps. A hand sewing needle which is medium in length with a small rounded eye. It is available in sizes 1 to 12. Assorted packages of needles sizes 5 to 10 are most useful. (The higher the number, the finer the needle.)

Paper, brown. Used on top of the wrong side of the leather when pressing and for pattern pieces.

Pattern hold. A pressurized spray which may be applied to the wrong side of the pattern making it pressure sensitive. Press the pattern against the skin with the hand and the pattern remains in position during cutting and marking. The spray will not stain.

Press cloth. Used dry for pressing on the wrong side of the leather.

Presser foot. A *roller* presser foot (Figure 17) for the sewing machine is excellent for top stitching to prevent the presser foot from sticking to the leather. A *teflon-coated* presser foot, available for some machines, is also an aid for stitching heavier leathers.

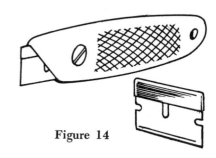

Figure 14

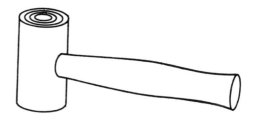

Figure 15

Figure 16

Figure 17

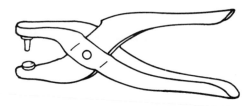

Figure 18

Punch pliers. A punch used to cut a hole for an eyelet for a worked buttonhole (Figure 18).

Ruler, square, yardstick, or tape measure. Used for measuring.

Sandpaper. Used to "shave" leather to make it thinner when covering buttons.

Stiletto. A pointed instrument used to shape the eyelet on a worked buttonhole.

Tape, mending. A *clear transparent tape* used for "basting" or holding leather together temporarily before stitching. *Cellophane tape* may be substituted, but it adheres to some leathers, taking off part of the surface nap when it is removed.

Thimble. A metal or plastic cover for the third finger of the right hand.

SUPPLIES

Belting. A skirt belting used at the top of skirts instead of a self-waistband.

Buttons. *Self-covered* buttons can be made successfully using "buttons to cover" kits with a rubber holder. Heavier leathers are "shaved" with sandpaper. The wrong side of coat suede may be used for the right side of buttons. *Costume* buttons which harmonize with the garment leather are also acceptable.

Closure (nylon tape). A nylon tape with a fleece and burr side (such as "Velcro") may be used as a closure for belts and waistbands, or to attach collars and cuffs.

Foundation cord. *Gimp, embroidery floss* or *yarn* used to pad a worked buttonhole.

Grosgrain ribbon. Grosgrain ribbon in various widths may be used for backing of skirt waistband in leather or suede skirts. It is also used for a facing substitute rather than using leather in front closures of weskits, jackets, etc.

Hook and eye. A large fastening for waistbands.

Interfacings. Fabric used between the garment and the facing to help an area retain its shape. A *lightweight hair canvas* may be used for capeskin coats and jackets, deerskin and garment suede. For lighter weight and softer skins, *nonwoven interfacing* may be used such as Pellon, or Interlon. A *woven interfacing* such as Siri or Formite may be substituted. For collars and cuffs, bias Pellon, organdy, or stiffened lawn is suggested.

Linings. The lining fabric should be durable, opaque, colorfast, and smooth. *Rayon twill* is very durable. *Rayon crepes, satins,* and *crepe-back satins* are also available. *Taffeta* is often used for skirt linings; *garment twill* or *sheath lining,* for vests, weskits, and sleeveless tops. *China silk, Touché,* and *Si Bonne* are excellent for the new sheer suedes.

Mending tape, iron-on. A colored material which can be ironed on a surface to reinforce weak areas. It is available in tapes of various widths or in small sheets.

Muslin. The garment is first made of muslin minus the facings. The muslin pattern is fitted and the necessary alterations are transferred to the paper pattern.

Shoulder pads. A lightweight shoulder pad may be used in some coat styles, but is optional.

Tape. A *silk* or *rayon bias* or *seam tape* is attached to the facing and hand stitched to the lining. Preshrunk ⅜ inch *linen tape* or seam tape is used to stay seams.

Tape, snap. A *twill tape* with snaps attached is used to make a detachable lining.

Thread. Matching thread of silk, *subsilk,* heavy-duty 2-to-3-ply *mercerized cotton, Dual Duty cotton,* or *"Taslon" nylon. Waxed-linen thread* suitable for hand sewing heavy leathers.

Zipper. A 7 to 9 inch *metal skirt zipper* is suitable for skirts, shorts, and vests. For zip-out linings, use a *separating zipper,* 80 inches or less in length depending on the coat size. The *Unique Invisible Zipper* in which the placket is not basted or pressed is an excellent choice for lightweight leather plackets.

4

PREPARING

TO SEW

SELECTING THE PATTERN

Dressmaker patterns are easily adaptable to leather provided the design is for heavier kinds of material (Figures 19 and 20). (See also p. 74.) Most slacks or short patterns are useable, as are skirt designs in either a straight or A-line design. Sometimes a center seam facilitates cutting, and omitting front facings might be necessary. For jerkins, weskits, and vests, regular patterns may be used with minor adjustments. Facings are often omitted and the garments are fully lined instead. Coat and jacket designs may feature set-in, kimono, dolman, or raglan sleeves (Figure 21). Collars may be shawl or convertible. Collarless garments can be enhanced by fur trim or a knitted band at the neckline. Buttons with bound or worked button-holes, loop or frog closures are suitable for leather garments. Almost any type of pocket may be utilized. Lining, attached or the zip-out type, may be made of fur, pile, quilted, or laminated fabrics. In full-length coats, center back seams and crosswise seams are sometimes necessary to use the leather to its best advantage. Such seams may be contrived to contribute to the attractiveness of the design. Jumpers, shifts, suits, and quilted parkas are high fashion items in sheer suede. Hat designs, like turbans, berets, and cloches, work up well in leather using the scrap pieces. Small purses, bags, and belts can also be made to complement your ensemble.

Combining leather with the heavier fabrics such as wool or a double knit can be very effective. Sometimes front panels in a jacket are used, or bindings or closure tabs. Leather buttons, yokes, or collars are often featured for contrast. Even hats may be trimmed with flowers and leaves of leather.

Select the same pattern size for a leather garment as you would for a fabric garment. Make the garment from muslin first. Alterations are made on the

Figure 19

Figure 20

muslin and transferred to the paper pattern. This is done because leather cannot be ripped successfully without leaving needle holes. If the garment is to be fully lined, making and fitting the lining first will eliminate the need for making a muslin pattern.

LAYING OUT THE PATTERN

"Grain" in leather refers to the outer layer of the animal's skin. It is the distinct pattern remaining after the hair has been removed. The grain, which is similar to warp or the lengthwise grain of fabric, runs along the backbone of an animal hide. All of the lengthwise grainline markings of the pattern pieces are laid parallel to this imaginary line so the garment will hang properly. The pattern pieces may be placed interchangeably with the top of one piece up and the bottom of another piece up, *except for suede which may have shading differences.* It is not advisable to cut pattern pieces on the crosswise grain because the leather tends to stretch.

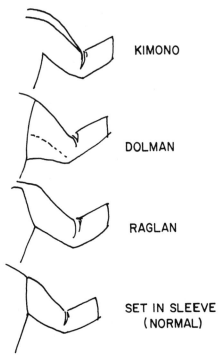

KIMONO

DOLMAN

RAGLAN

SET IN SLEEVE
(NORMAL)

Figure 21

REMEMBER: Leather has no straight or bias; it stretches but it does not shrink.

Equipment.

Pattern showing fitting alterations.

Ball-point pen or wax chalk.

Mending tape, weights, or pins.

Yardstick, ruler, or square.

Iron-on mending tape (optional).

Brown paper.

Procedure. (NOTE: Cobraskin must be pieced before cutting. See p. 20.)

Examine the skin for weak spots and imperfections.

1. Press iron-on mending tape on the wrong side of the skin over the thin spots.
2. Mark scuffs or imperfections on wrong side with a ball-point pen or chalk.
3. Notice the thickness and thinness of each skin. The neck of the hide is usually the thickest.

Prepare the pattern for layout.

1. Make all alterations from the fitted muslin on the paper pattern.
2. *Trim the pattern seams to ⅜ inch except when a welt seam will be used or when top stitching more than ¼ inch from the edge.*
3. Make a brown paper pattern for all pieces which are to be placed on the fold or for which "cut two" is indicated. In other words, you will need two side fronts, two sleeves, and so forth.
4. Join the brown paper half and the pattern half together at the fold line for pieces which indicate "place on fold."

Place the pattern on the wrong side of the skin.

1. Keep in mind that a skin's greatest strength is in the center. Cut the parts which will get the hardest wear from the center sections.
2. Use the best matched pieces for the front and sleeves.
3. Place the pattern pieces on the leather, adjusting them to avoid imperfect spots in the skin.
4. Keep the lengthwise grainline of the pattern parallel to the backbone of the animal skin.
5. Try to have equal thicknesses of leather on related areas of the finished garment.
6. Be sure to match the markings when using fake skins such as reptile and alligator.
7. *Pay attention to shading differences when using suede. All pieces must be laid in the same direction with the top of the pattern toward the neck end.*
8. *Never cut leather folded or on the crosswise grain.*

Attach pattern to the skin (Figure 22).

1. Pattern holder may be used (p. 14).
2. Mending tape is excellent for attaching the pattern because it does not tear the pattern as easily as cellophane tape when it is removed. Tape in as many places as necessary.
3. Pattern may be pinned if pins are placed in the seam allowance.
4. Weights (fishing sinkers are handy) may also be used to hold the pattern in place.
5. Plan where piecings will be made if they are necessary. *Do not* piece near major construction seams such as the waist, sleeve, and neck seams. Plan pieces to enhance the design of the garment.
6. Omit facings on completely lined garments. Grosgrain ribbon may be substituted for facings on suit and

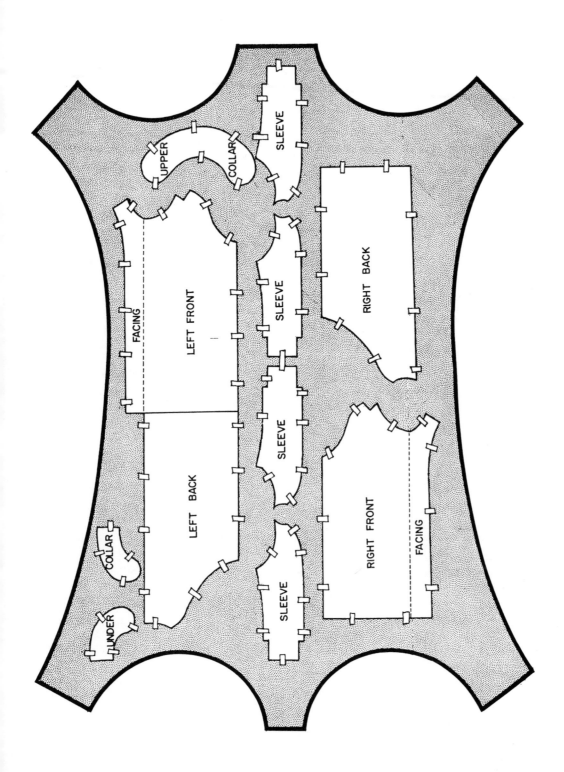

Figure 22

coat fronts and for waistband backing on skirts and shorts.

7. Check the lengthwise grain of pattern from the backbone line of the skins with a square or a yardstick.

Preparation of Cobra Before Cutting

Cobra must be pieced before cutting. The backbone pattern has darker scales at the wide end of the skin which fade out toward the narrow end. Center the pattern and cut the skin into equal strips. Sew pieces of the cobra together to fit the pattern pieces. The backbone pattern may be pieced to create a border effect by placing the darker scales next to each other. Another effect may be created by placing the dark pattern at the top on one skin and on the bottom of the adjacent skin.

Preparation of Quilted Suede

1. Quilt the suede before cutting out the pattern.
2. Place one thickness of cotton wadding or dacron fiberfill against the wrong side of the suede. Place a lightweight backing (lining fabric) over the wadding.
3. Plan the quilting pattern. You may use a quilting guide for the machine or draw lines on paper. Use paper that can be removed easily after stitching.
4. Stitch through all thicknesses using from eight to ten stitches an inch.

CUTTING OUT THE LEATHER OR SUEDE GARMENT

Sewing with leather or suede is not difficult, but requires a little time and patience. As mistakes are not easily corrected, check the list of questions below before cutting. Most garment leather may be cut with an ordinary dressmaker's shears, 7½ to 8 inches in length. A razor blade or furrier's knife may be used for heavier leather.

Equipment.
Shears, 7½ to 8 inches.

Furrier's leather knife or a razor blade.

Procedure.
Check before cutting.

1. Are the pattern pieces placed on the wrong side of the skin?
2. Are all pieces laid on the lengthwise grain (parallel to the backbone of the animal)?
3. Is the leather laid out flat, not folded?
4. Are all seam allowances on the pattern trimmed to ⅜ inch? (NOTE: Do not trim if welt seams are to be used or if top stitching is over ¼ inch from edge.)
5. Have all fitting alterations been transferred to the paper pattern?
6. Are duplicates cut from brown paper for the pattern pieces which indicate "cut two"? Is a complete pattern cut when it indicates "place on fold"?
7. Is the thickness and the thinness of the leather evenly distributed among the pattern pieces?
8. Are the best matched pieces used for the front and sleeves?
9. *If using suede, are all pieces laid in one direction?*

Cut out the garment.

1. Cut with a shears using long, even strokes. Avoid jagged edges.
2. Place one hand on the pattern and cut around to the right of the pattern.
3. Cut notches outward wherever necessary.
4. You may prefer to trace the complete pattern with a ball-point pen or chalk before cutting.

5. Heavier leathers may be cut with a furrier's knife (razor blade in a holder) or a sharp single-edge razor blade. Cut straight lines along a ruler on a board.

MARKING THE LEATHER OR SUEDE

Traditional methods of marking (tailor tacks, tracing wheel, and dressmaker's carbon), used in dressmaking for transferring construction details to the garment, cannot be used for leather since they would leave holes in the skin.

Equipment.
Ball-point pen.

Wax chalk.

Mending tape.

Straightedge.

Procedure.
Transfer construction details to the underside of the skin.

1. Transfer all necessary markings such as fold line, darts, fashion detail lines, seam lines on collar, cuffs, welts, pockets, buttonholes, and center front on garments with front closures.
2. On light-colored skins, markings may be transferred with a ball-point pen or wax chalk.
3. On black or dark leather, mending tape may be used for construction guidelines (Figure 23).

Transfer markings by lifting a portion of the pattern and folding it back along the line to be marked (Figure 24). Mark along the folded line. Use a ruler as a guideline for straight lines such as darts and buttonholes.

Alter pattern seam lines which form corners. Since corners cannot be turned successfully in leather or suede, alter the seam lines so the stitching line is slightly rounded, for example the corners of collars, cuffs, belts, lapels, and pockets.

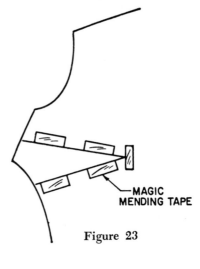

—MAGIC MENDING TAPE

Figure 23

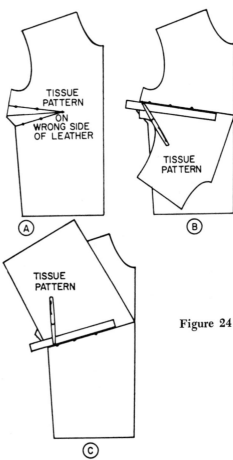

TISSUE PATTERN ON WRONG SIDE OF LEATHER

TISSUE PATTERN

(A)

(B)

TISSUE PATTERN

(C)

Figure 24

5

SEWING LEATHER AND SUEDE

Leather and suede are no more difficult to sew than fabric. In some instances they are even more manageable since they do not slip under the presser foot.

Stitching.

Machine stitching. (NOTE: Be sure your machine is free from oil.)

Use a leather-point needle (15 by 2) which is particularly designed for stitching leather. The wedge point makes a clean cut in the leather resulting in a uniform stitch.

1. For lightweight leathers, kidskin, fine capeskin, and sheer suedes, use a size 11 needle.
2. For medium-weight leathers, garment suede, lambskin, and capeskin, use a size 14 needle.
3. For heavyweight leathers, heavier capeskin, lambskin, or multiple layers, use a size 16 needle.

Adjust the length of the machine stitch by testing on a scrap of leather.

1. Generally, seven to ten stitches per inch are used.
2. Sheer suedes and soft, pliable leathers may use as many as twelve stitches per inch.
3. Heavy leathers use seven to eight stitches per inch.
4. In topstitching, a few more stitches per inch will improve appearances.

Check the pressure regulator (Figure 25). Leather and suede are thicker and spongier than fabric so less pressure needs to be applied with the presser foot. Loosen it if necessary.

Check the upper tension (Figure 25). Lower tensions seldom need adjustment.

1. If the thread is too loose and loops form on the bottom of the seam, tighten the tension.

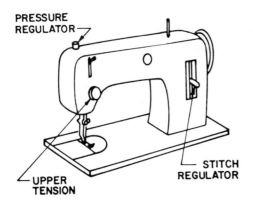

PRESSURE
REGULATOR

UPPER
TENSION

STITCH
REGULATOR

Figure 25

2. If the thread breaks or loops on top of the seam, loosen the tension.

Stitch accurately since ripped seams leave holes in the leather.

Use a roller-presser foot or teflon-coated foot, especially for topstitching.

Use one of the following types of thread:

1. Silk thread is excellent for leather because of its elasticity and tensile strength.
2. Subsilk works well since it is a mercerized cotton. It is chemically treated to make it stronger, more receptive to dyes, and lustrous in imitation of silk thread.
3. A 2- or 3-ply heavy-duty mercerized or Dual Duty thread may also be used.

4. Texturized nylon thread has elasticity. However, some synthetic threads pick up lint due to static electricity and sometimes fray.

Hand stitching.

Use a glover's needle.
Use one of the following types of thread:

1. On lightweight leathers, use silk, subsilk, or 2- to 3-ply heavy-duty mercerized thread.
2. Run the thread through beeswax to keep it from snarling. The thread will also slip through the leather more easily.
3. Silk buttonhole twist may be used for fashion details on the right side of leathers.
4. For sheepskin jackets, the seams may be sewn by hand with a waxed, heavy linen thread.

Running stitch (Figure 26).

1. The running stitch is used for basting seams in the lining. It is also used for sewing seams in heavy leathers.
2. Push the needle in and out of the fabric or leather, taking several small stitches at a time before pulling the threads through.

Backstitch (Figure 27).

1. The backstitch is used for stitching seams by hand when it is difficult to reach them by machine. It resembles a machine stitch.

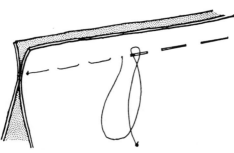

Figure 26

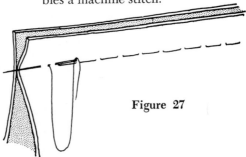

Figure 27

2. Take a stitch from right to left. Point the needle toward the left, bringing it up twice the length of the finished stitch. Continue in the same manner, inserting the needle close to the last stitch and bringing it up twice the length of the stitch.

Uneven backstitch.

1. The uneven backstitch is made the same way as a backstitch, except that the needle is carried a portion of the stitch each time.
2. The uneven backstitch is used to sew zippers in by hand in soft leathers.
3. When the needle is carried back just a few yarns, the stitch is called a *prick* stitch.

Slip stitch.

1. The slip stitch is used to hem free bottom linings in coats, skirts, vests, and weskits.
2. Bring the thread up through the edge of the hem, sewing from right to left.
3. Take a tiny stitch in the garment opposite this point. The stitch will be close to the fold and perpendicular to the hem (Figure 28, A).
4. Insert the needle in the hem fold; slip it along inside the fold for the desired stitch length and repeat (Figure 28, B).

Basting.

You may baste with rubber cement (Figure 29, A). It can be lifted and adjusted on most leathers. Test a sample first.

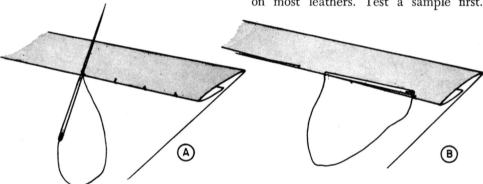

Figure 28

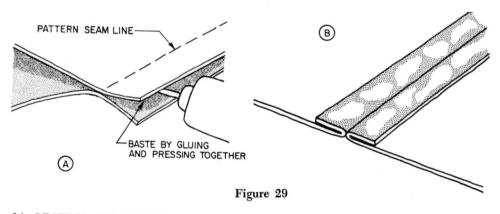

PATTERN SEAM LINE

BASTE BY GLUING AND PRESSING TOGETHER

Figure 29

Care must be taken not to get glue outside of seam allowance (Figure 29, B). Also, rubber cement may gum up a sewing machine if much stitching is done over it. See p. 49 for glue removal.

Seams can be clipped with paper clips, but care must be taken not to scuff the leather (Figure 30).

Seams can be held together with mending tape (Figure 31).

Seams may be pinned if the pins are placed well outside of the stitching line.

Seams.

REMEMBER: Seams cannot be let out, so if in doubt, make it large and take it in. Round all corners to eliminate bulk in turning. Use directional stitching, i.e., stitch from the highest to the lowest points or from the widest to the narrowest. Tie the threads; do not retrace since this cuts the leather.

Plain seaming.

1. Baste the seam with one of the above methods.
2. Apply preshrunk *linen tape* or *rayon seam tape* on top of the seams to keep them from stretching, particularly at points of strain (Figure 32).
3. Ease the leather into the machine under the presser foot slowly, guiding the tape with one hand and the leather with the other, being careful not to stretch the leather.

NOTE: Seams in heavy sheepskin are sewn by hand with a tight running stitch, using a glover's needle and waxed-linen thread. In thicker parts of the skin, it may be necessary to pierce holes with an awl or to pull the needle through with a small pair of pliers.
4. When joining leather and cloth, stitch with the cloth on top.
5. Fasten threads by tying at the end with a square knot. *Do not* backstitch as it will cut the leather.
6. Skive seam edges making a graded or beveled edge to reduce bulk.
   a) On lightweight leathers, make a skive seam edge by trimming with a sharp shears held at an angle (Figure 33).

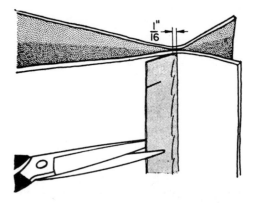

Figure 32

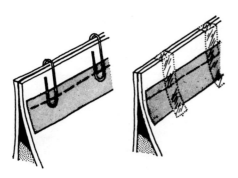

Figure 30   **Figure 31**

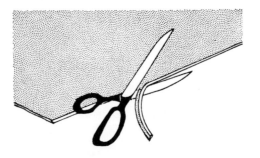

Figure 33

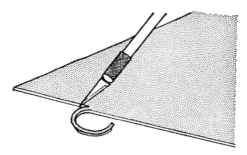

Figure 34

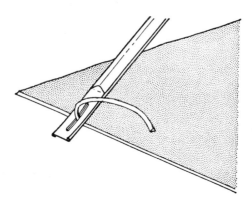

Figure 35

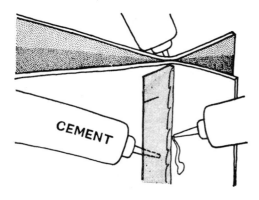

CEMENT

Figure 36

b) Make the skive with an X-acto knife (Figure 34) or a safety beveler (Figure 35).

7. Snip tape at intervals along the edges (Figure 32).

8. Press with a warm iron, first as stitched and then with the seam open. Use brown paper or a press cloth between the leather and the iron. *Never use steam.*

9. Apply rubber cement with a brush, syringe, or applicator to the tape and the seam allowance of the leather (Figure 36).

10. Press the seam down with your fingers for sheer suedes and lighter weight leathers, and pound it with a mallet for cowhide and heavier leather. Allow it to dry (Figure 37).

11. Lift the seam up lightly. It will now lie flat with less tension and pull.

12. A plain seam may be topstitched (see p. 27) by turning (press, glue, and pound) both seam allowances in the same direction and topstitching the desired distance from the seam line (Figure 38).

13. A plain seam may be double topstitched by opening the seam (press, glue, and pound) and topstitching the desired width from the seam line on each side (Figure 39).

Crossing seams.

1. When seams cross, press, glue, and pound them so they lie flat.

2. Lift and trim the corners of the seams to remove bulk.

Grading seams.

1. Grading refers to trimming seams to different widths after stitching.

2. Interfacings are always trimmed close to the line of stitching.

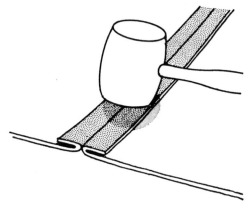

Figure 37

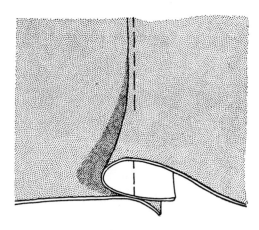

Figure 38

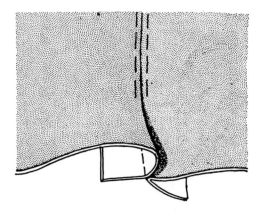

Figure 39

3. The seam pressed toward the right side of the garment is left somewhat longer to cushion the other seam. For example, the coat front seams are wider than the facing seams; the lapel facing seams are wider than the coat seams; the upper collar seams are wider than the under collar seams; the upper flap (pocket) seams are wider than the under flap seams.

Skiving seams.

1. Skiving refers to the reduction of the leather's thickness.
2. The cut edges of a seam may be skived by use of a sharp shears, X-acto knife or a safety beveler.
3. See "Seams," p. 25, Plain seaming, 6.

Topstitching seams.

1. Before topstitching, be sure the seams are graded, the corners rounded and all excess bulk removed.
2. Press and pound the seams lightly.
3. Check the desired stitches per inch on scrap leather and then topstitch.
4. Use a *roller-presser foot* or *teflon-coated foot* when topstitching. *Saran Wrap* or *tissue paper* may be placed under the regular presser foot to prevent slippage.

Curving seams.

1. Small triangular pieces are removed from curved seams to reduce bulk. This can be done with the points of a sharp shears or X-acto knife. Curving is done before the seams are cemented. Curving will be necessary on such seams as pocket, armhole, and crotch (Figure 40).

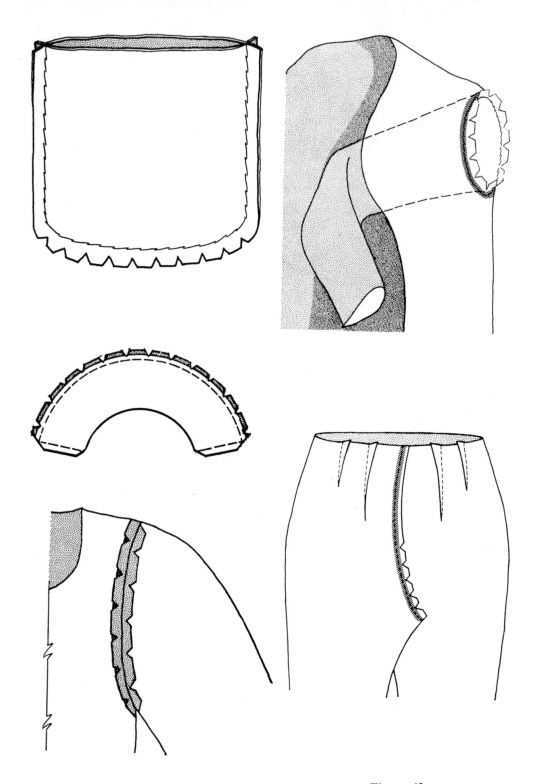

Figure 40

Welt seams.

1. The welt seam is most commonly used for jackets and coats. It is also used instead of flat-felled seams for tailored leather shirts.
2. Make a plain seam on the wrong side of the garment.
3. Trim the seam edge next to the garment about $\frac{1}{16}$ to $\frac{1}{8}$ inch (Figure 41, A).
4. Turn both edges to the same side; press, glue, and pound them.
5. Stitch on the right side the desired distance from the seam line (Figure 41, B). The stitching catches the raw edge of one side of the seam.

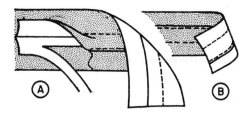

Figure 41

Lap seams.

1. The lap seam is used for yokes or to piece leather in design features.
2. Turn one edge of the leather under. Glue and pound the edge.
3. Lap the turned edge onto the other edge. The raw edges, the marked seam line, and the turned edge meet (Figure 42).
4. Stitch on the right side the desired distance from the fold.

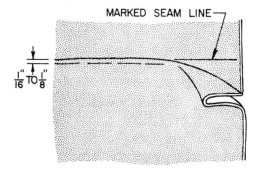

Figure 42

Slot seams.

1. A slot seam is decorative. It functions effectively when it is necessary to piece skins. The slot seam can be used for a cross seam or a center back seam in a coat or center front seam of a skirt.
2. Fold the seam along both cut edges and turn under. Glue and pound it.
3. Glue over the underlay, either folding the edges together or keeping them slightly apart as you wish (Figure 43).
4. Stitch as far as desired from the folded edge.

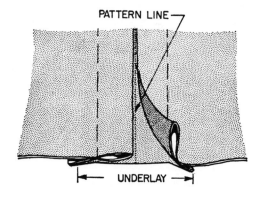

Figure 43

Piped seam edge.

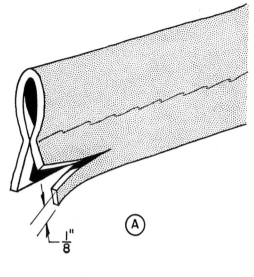

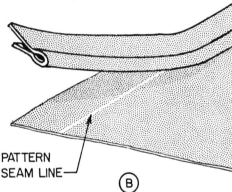

PATTERN
SEAM LINE

1. The piped seam edge is a European style of piping used for coat and jacket fronts, crosswise seams, around pocket flaps and the bottom of sleeves.
2. Cut a strip of leather piping and stitch the desired width from the folded edge. Trim ⅛ inch from one side (Figure 44, A).
3. Place the piping on the right side of the garment with the piping stitching on top of the seam line. Stitch along the piping stitching (Figure 44, B).
4. Fold the piping-garment seam back so that the folded edge of the piping extends outward.
5. Lay the wrong side of the facing (or piece to be attached) against the wrong side of the garment, matching the seam lines.
6. Stitch from the right side in the groove through all thicknesses (Figure 44, C).
7. Cut off the raw edge of the facing as closely as desired (Figure 44, D).

   SUGGESTION: On a suede garment, the piping may be made with the wrong side of the leather (smooth) out for contrast.

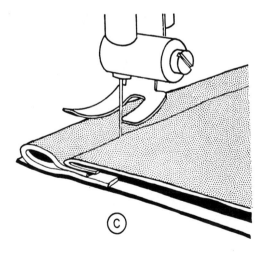

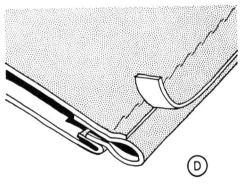

Figure 44

Piped seam, reinforced.

1. The reinforced piped seam is used for piping on the bottom of sleeves, around cardigan necklines, and down the front closures of coats and jackets. It is also used for crosswise seams.
2. Cut a strip of leather piping the desired width. Fold it in half and press it. Stitch the piping the desired width.
3. Lay the folded strip on the right side of the leather with the raw edges together. Sew by machine about 1/4 inch from the edge (Figure 45, A).
4. Place the other piece of leather on top with the wrong side up and stitch again, making the seam a little deeper, about 3/8 inch (Figure 45, B).

Facing seams.

To prevent seam from rolling out of place, glue seam allowances.

Leather-lining seams (when no facings are used).

To keep the lining from extending beyond the seam, glue the leather side of the seam allowance in position. A small running stitch with matching thread may be used near the edge of the lining seam edge.

Darts.

Stitch the dart along the marked line. Tie the threads. *Do not retrace* (Figure 46).

Cut out the extra leather, leaving a seam width of 3/8 inch on the sides and near the point (Figure 47).

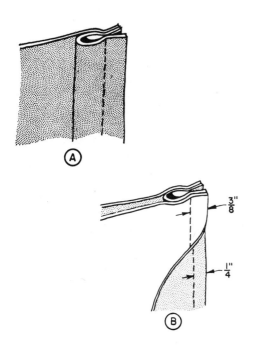

Figure 45

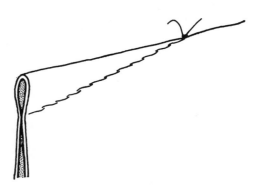

Figure 46

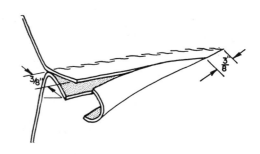

Figure 47

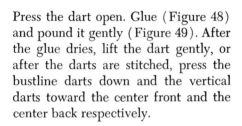

Figure 48

Press the dart open. Glue (Figure 48) and pound it gently (Figure 49). After the glue dries, lift the dart gently, or after the darts are stitched, press the bustline darts down and the vertical darts toward the center front and the center back respectively.

Cut along the fold line of the dart to within ⅜ inch from the point (Figure 50).

Cut from the wide end of the dart through the top layer to within ⅜ inch of the point.

Remove the triangular piece (NOTE: Small darts need not be trimmed, but pressed toward the center).

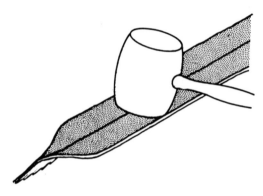

Figure 49

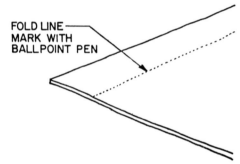

FOLD LINE
MARK WITH
BALLPOINT PEN

Figure 51

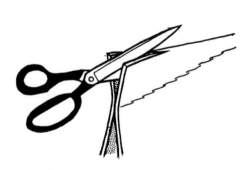

Figure 50

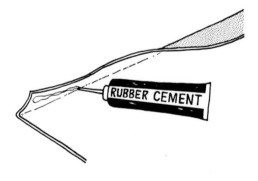

Figure 52

Hems.

Mark the fold line of the hem with a ball-point pen on the wrong side of the leather (Figure 51).

Apply rubber cement as far as the fold line to the wrong sides of the hem and to about one-half inch below the top of the hemline. (Figure 52).

Fold the hem up, pressing it with your fingers. Pound it gently with the mallet (Figure 53), or press with the iron and brown paper.

On curved hems, small triangular pieces should be removed at the cut edge so the hem lies flat (Figure 54).

It is usually suggested that the hems be no less than 1 inch and no more than 2 inches in width. Or hems may be *lapstitched* with one or two rows of topstitching.

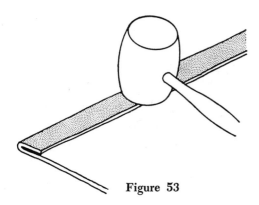

Figure 53

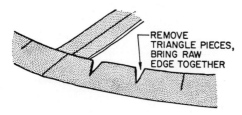

REMOVE TRIANGLE PIECES, BRING RAW EDGE TOGETHER

Figure 54

6

CLOSURES FOR LEATHER AND SUEDE GARMENTS

Although some people desire to have a leather or suede garment in a wrap-around style, one need not avoid closures because of imagined difficulty. In this chapter, bound buttonholes, worked buttonholes, nylon tape closures, zippers, loops, and frogs are discussed. Machine-worked buttonholes may also be made. On some sewing machines it is possible to pad the buttonhole with a foundation cord of embroidery floss.

BOUND BUTTONHOLES

Bound buttonholes are as easily constructed on leather or suede garments as on fabric. A sample buttonhole should be prepared first.

Procedure.
Mark the placement of the buttonhole.

1. Use a ball-point pen on the wrong side to mark the length of the buttonhole.
2. The length of the buttonhole is determined by measuring the diameter of the button plus one thickness of the button.
3. Mark a rectangle with a ball-point pen the desired length and ¼ inch to ⁵⁄₁₆ inch wide (Figure 55).

   NOTE: On stretchy leathers it is desirable to stitch the marked rectangular shape.

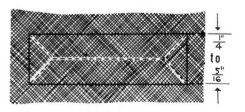

Figure 55

Prepare the buttonhole opening.

1. Using a sharp scissors, slash the buttonhole on the marked buttonhole line to ⅜ inch from the end.
2. Clip diagonally to the corners leaving a triangle at each end.
3. Turn triangles and side strips to the inside on the rectangular markings (Figure 56) and press.

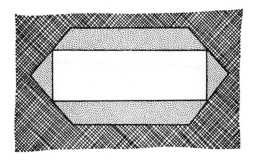

Figure 56

Prepare the buttonhole strips.

1. Cut two leather strips for each buttonhole, slightly longer than the buttonhole and about 1½ inches wide.
2. Fold the strips lengthwise, right sides out, with one side ¼ inch shorter than the other side (Figure 57) and press. You may stitch strip ⅛ inch plus from the folded edge.

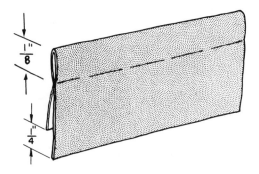

Figure 57

Attach the strip to the garment.

1. Holding the right side of the garment up, place a prepared strip lengthwise in the opening with the widest part of the strip toward the wrong side of the garment (Figure 58).
2. Hold the strip in position with mending tape.

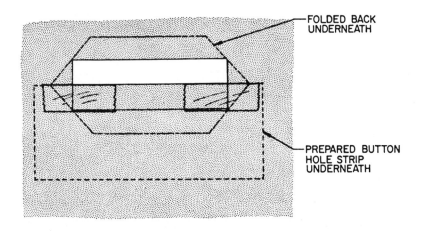

FOLDED BACK
UNDERNEATH

PREPARED BUTTON
HOLE STRIP
UNDERNEATH

Figure 58

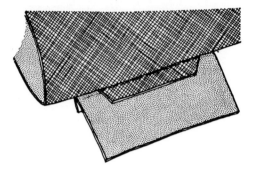

Figure 59

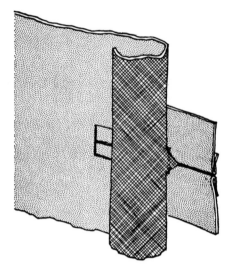

Figure 60

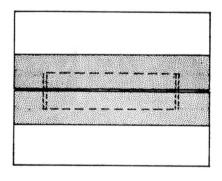

Figure 61

3. Lifting the garment up, stitch along the marked buttonhole line, attaching the clipped strip which was turned inside to the binding strip (Figure 59). Do not stitch through the face of the garment.
4. Repeat this procedure with the other binding strip.

Finish the ends of the buttonhole.

1. Fold back the garment at the end of the buttonhole, right sides together, exposing the triangle.
2. Stitch at the base of the triangle, attaching it to the two binding strips (Figure 60). Stitch at least two separate rows (Figure 61).

Apply the facing to the buttonhole (*this is done after the facing is attached to the garment*).

Lining or cloth facing:

1. Mark a rectangle with a ball-point pen which is the area of the finished buttonhole as described on p. 34.
2. Using a sharp scissors, slash and clip the buttonhole and turn back the edges as on p. 35.
3. Hand stitch the rectangle in the lining facing to the leather.

Leather facing:

1. Stitch a rectangle around the outside of the buttonhole from the right side.
2. Trim the leather facing close to the line of stitching.

Simplified Bound Buttonhole.

1. Place a small piece of suede on the wrong side of the garment over the buttonhole area.

2. Mark the length of the buttonhole.
3. Stitch around the marking about ⅛ inch from the marked line.

   NOTE: Bound buttonholes may be made in lightweight leathers or suede by using the Dritz Bound Buttonhole Maker.
4. Slash on the marked line.

WORKED BUTTONHOLES

The handworked buttonhole may be used on coats, leather jackets, sport coats, and shirts.

Equipment.
   Punch pliers or buttonhole cutter.

   Scissors.

   Glover's needle.

   Foundation cord such as gimp, embroidery floss, or yarn.

   Buttonhole twist.

   Beeswax.

   Stiletto or orange stick.

Procedure.
Mark the position of the buttonhole with a ball-point pen or mending tape.

Cut the buttonhole.

1. Using punch pliers, cut the eyelet on the center front end of the buttonhole.
2. Cut the remainder of the buttonhole line.

   NOTE: The eyelet can be cut with the point of a sharp scissors. Some buttonhole cutters cut the eyelet and the opening in one operation.

Pad the buttonhole with foundation end.

1. To pad the buttonhole, use gimp or a substitute twice the length of the buttonhole.
2. Place a knot in one end and bring it up toward the eyelet end of the buttonhole along the cut edge of the wrong side (Figure 62, A).
3. Tape it into position.

Prepare the twist.

1. Use buttonhole twist to match the leather.
2. Allow about 1 yard of twist for a 1 inch buttonhole.
3. Draw the twist gently over the beeswax, and then between absorbent paper or a cloth and a warm iron.
4. Waxing prevents the twist from knotting and snarling.

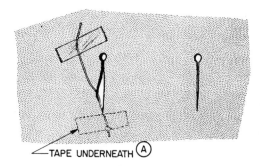

TAPE UNDERNEATH (A)

Figure 62

Work the buttonhole stitch.

1. Hold the garment in one hand with the eyelet away from you.
2. Bring the needle through the opening and at right angles, pushing it only halfway through the leather.

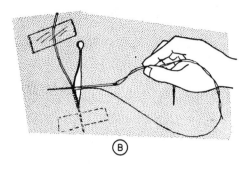

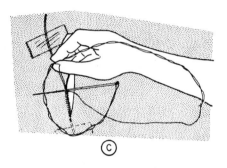

Figure 62

Figure 63

Holding your thumbnail close to the stitching line will help to guide the stitch depth.

3. Grasp the double thread near the eye of the needle (Figure 62, B) and cross it, passing it under the point of the needle from right to left (Figure 62, C).

4. Pull the needle out and directly upward almost to the end.

5. Grasp the thread between the thumb and index finger, pulling the thread toward you and then away to set the purl.

6. Keep the foundation cord on top of the cut edge, working the stitch over it.

7. Continue the buttonhole stitch to the bar end, ending exactly opposite the first stitch taken.

Fasten the foundation cord.

1. Draw up the foundation cord. Hold a stiletto or a large matchstick at the eyelet to shape it.

2. Fasten it by gluing it on the wrong side of the garment.

Work the bar end.

1. Make a bar of three or four stitches (Figure 63).

2. Have each stitch extend from the depth of a stitch on one side to the depth of a stitch on the other side.

NYLON TAPE CLOSURES

A nylon tape closure is a flat, secure, adjustable closure which may be used to fasten belts, waistbands, jackets, and sleeve cuffs, or to attach accessories. The tape has a fleece side and a burr side which adhere to each other. It is about an inch wide and is available in most of the basic colors.

Procedure.
Prepare the tape.

1. Cut the tape to the desired length and width.

2. Press the closed tape flat with a moderately warm iron.

3. Separate the two sides of the tape by pulling them apart (Figure 64).

Attach the burr side of the tape.

1. Using mending tape, attach the burr side of the tape, right side up, to the lower part of the closing.
2. Place the burr side about ⅛ inch inside of the seam line (Figure 65, A).
3. Using a zipper foot, machine stitch along the outside edges.

Attach the fleece side of the tape.

1. Using mending tape, attach the fleece side, right side up, on the top part of the closing exactly opposite the lower closing.
2. Place the tape about ⅛ inch from the seam line (Figure 65, B).
3. Machine stitch it into position, using a zipper foot along the outside edges.

    NOTE: For a custom look, the stitching may be done by hand using a buttonhole twist, glover's needle, and an uneven backstitch.

    If nylon tape is used on a garment with a facing, the fleece side may be stitched on the right side of the facing before the facing is attached to the garment so that the stitches will not show on the outside of the garment.

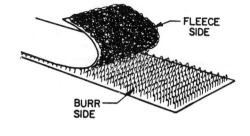

Figure 64

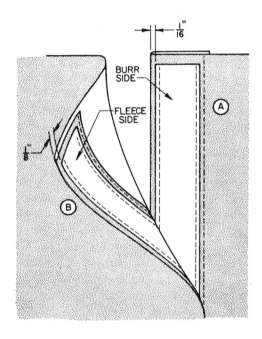

Figure 65

ZIPPERS

The zipper is the most commonly used closure today. It may be attached with the lapped edge or set into a slot seam. In the slot-seam method, the zipper is inserted with two folds meeting over the metal. It may be used for jacket or coat closures, sleeve plackets, skirt plackets, or neckline openings. The methods used for attaching zippers to leather varies slightly from the methods used for fabric. After completing the closure, the raw edge of the suede may be glued to the garment for a flatter finish.

Slot-Seam Zippers.
Points to check before attaching the zipper:

1. Be sure the garment is properly fitted.
2. When measuring for the placket opening, measure from the top stop to the bottom of the zipper *plus* the seam allowance, *plus* 1/16 inch.

Baste the placket opening.

1. Fold back the placket opening along the seam line and press.
2. Baste the placket closed with mending tape by placing strips of tape crosswise over the opening on the right side of the leather. Be sure the seam line folds meet (Figure 66, A).

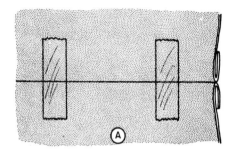

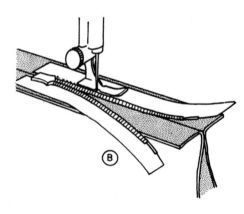

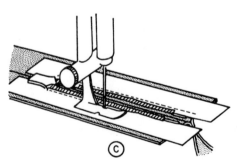

Figure 66

Attach the zipper to the seam allowance.

1. Put the zipper foot on the machine.
2. Open the zipper and place it face down with the bottom stop and pull tab at the end of the placket. Be sure that a seam allowance plus $\frac{1}{16}$ inch remains above the top stop.
3. Stitch the zipper tape to the *seam allowance* from the bottom up. Begin at the top of the pull tab with the edge of the teeth on the seam line (Figure 66, B).
4. Repeat on the other side of the zipper on the opposite seam allowance (Figure 66, C).

Stitch the zipper to the garment.

1. Close the zipper with the center face down on the seam line.
2. Spread the garment flat.
3. Stitch the zipper to the garment beginning at the top on one side. Stitch down, across the end, and up the other side (Figure 67, A).
4. Carefully remove the mending tape from the right side of the placket (Figure 67, B).

Lapped-Edge Zippers.
See [I] under "Slot-Seam Zippers," p. 39.

Prepare the placket opening.

1. Fold back the upper part of the closing along the seam line and press.
2. Fold back the lower part of the closing about $\frac{1}{8}$ inch beyond the seam line and press (Figure 68).
3. The folds form a small pleat in the seam allowance. Clip the seam if the pleat is too bulky.

Attach one side of the zipper to the lower placket opening.

1. Open the zipper.
2. With the right side of the garment

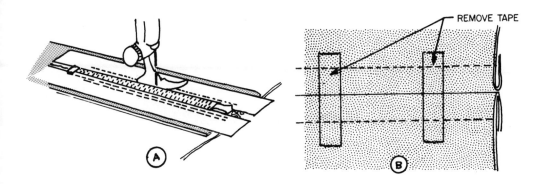

Figure 67

up and the zipper face up, place the back of the zipper tape under the opening with the fold close to the edge of the zipper teeth (Figure 69).

3. Be sure that a seam allowance plus $\frac{1}{16}$ inch remains above the top of the metal zipper.

4. Stitch from the bottom up, with a zipper foot, close to the edge of the fold.

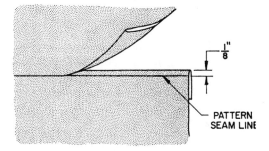

Figure 68

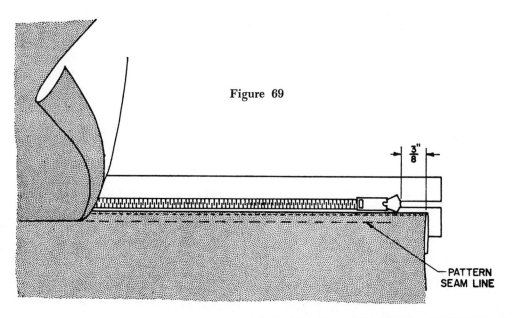

Figure 69

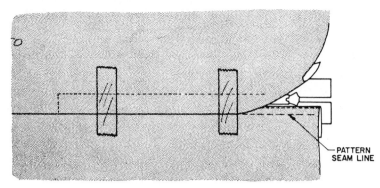

PATTERN
SEAM LINE

Figure 70

Attach the other side of the zipper to the upper lap of the placket opening.

1. Close the zipper.
2. Using mending tape, baste the upper lapped edge on top of the marked seam line on the lower opening (Figure 70).
3. Spread the garment flat. From the right side, stitch the zipper to the garment beginning at the bottom seam line across the bottom, pivot, and then stitch along the side close to the zipper teeth up to the top.
4. Remove the mending tape.

Invisible Zippers.
The invisible, or hidden seam zipper is easy to sew in with a special zipper foot. (See "Suppliers for Miscellaneous Items," p. 65.) There is no machine sewing on the right side—the hidden seam zipper. The placket need not be basted or pressed. Before attaching the zipper:

1. Be sure garment is properly fitted.
2. When measuring for the placket opening, measure from the top stop to the bottom of the zipper, *plus* the seam allowance, *plus* $\frac{1}{16}$ inch.
3. Put special zipper foot on machine.
4. Be sure the seam allowance is $\frac{3}{8}$ inch wide.

Attaching the zipper.

1. Open the zipper completely.
2. Place the zipper face down on the right side of the leather.
3. Match the edge of the tape exactly with the edge of the seam allowance.
4. Be sure the zipper teeth fall on the desired seam allowance.
5. Lower the zipper foot over the chain and stitch until the zipper foot touches the pull tab (Figure 71, A). Tie the threads.
6. Using the other groove of the foot, stitch the other half of the zipper in the same manner (Figure 71, B).

Complete the bottom of the zipper.

1. Close the zipper.
2. Close the bottom between the finished seam and the zipper by hand with the backstitch. An alternate method is to place the closed zipper on its side and sew the opening closed with a cording foot (Figure 71, C), or, close the seam as far as the zipper foot stitches and allow approximately 1 inch of the zipper to remain inside the placket.

NOTE: The zipper may be attached before the seam is made.

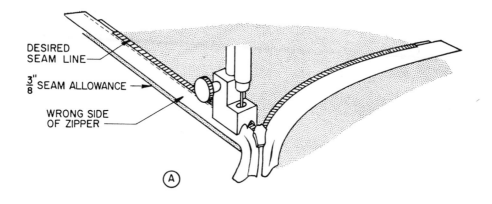

DESIRED
SEAM LINE

$\frac{3}{8}''$ SEAM ALLOWANCE

WRONG SIDE
OF ZIPPER

(A)

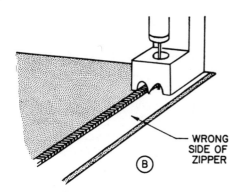

WRONG
SIDE OF
ZIPPER

(B)

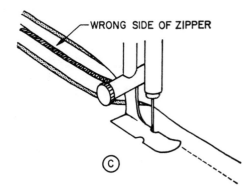

WRONG SIDE OF ZIPPER

(C)

Figure 71

COVERING BUTTONS IN LEATHER

Buttons may be covered in leather for a leather garment or for contrast on a fabric garment. Covered-button kits may be used successfully, particularly the type with a rubber holder. Heavier leather must be buffed with sandpaper on the back to make it thinner and more pliable.

Retailers use a line number to determine the size of buttons. Forty lines equal 1 inch.

Line
  18—⅜ inch
  20—½ inch
  24—⅝ inch
  30—¾ inch (size of dime)
  36—⅞ inch (size of nickel)
  40—1 inch (size of quarter)
  45—1⅛ inches
  55—1¾ inches
  60—1½ inches (size of silver dollar)
  70—1¾ inches
  75—1⅞ inches
  80—2 inches
  100—2½ inches

SEWING ON THE BUTTON

Procedure.
Locate the position of the button.

1. Lap the garment properly, center on top of center.

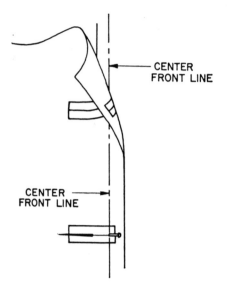

CENTER FRONT LINE

CENTER FRONT LINE

Figure 72

Figure 73

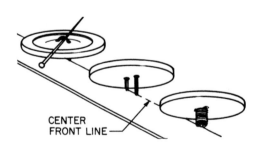

CENTER FRONT LINE

Figure 74

2. Mark the under closing at the outer end of the buttonhole (Figure 72).
3. Place the center of the button on this point.

Use buttonhole twist or heavy waxed thread and a glover's needle to sew on the button.

Sew on the *button without a shank.*

1. Take a stitch on the right side of the garment where the button is to be placed.
2. Place a pin on top of the button.
3. Bring the needle up through one hole of the button over the pin and through another hole to the wrong side of the leather (Figure 73).
4. Repeat until enough strands are present for durability.
5. Bring the thread up under the button. Remove the pin, pull the button up, and wind the thread between the button and the leather to form a shank.
6. Fasten the thread on the wrong side with several small stitches.

Sew on the *button with a shank.*

1. See steps described in "Locate the position of the button."
2. Sew by bringing the needle through the fabric and the shank, then back through the leather.
3. Keep the stitches small and parallel to the edge of the garment. This places the strain on the shank (Figure 74).

Sew on a *button with a stay button.*

1. Most jacket and coat buttons on garments receiving hard wear have a small button (stay) placed directly underneath the top button on the facing side (Figure 75).

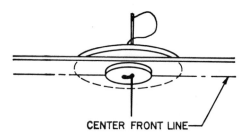

CENTER FRONT LINE

Figure 75

2. First, locate the position of the button, as explained on p. 43.
3. Sew *both buttons* on in one operation.

OTHER CLOSURES

Other types of closure which may be used are enclosed leather or braid loops (Figure 76, A), leather tabs (Figure 76, B), frogs (Figure 76, C), buckles (Figure 76, D), and dog leash (Figure 76, E).

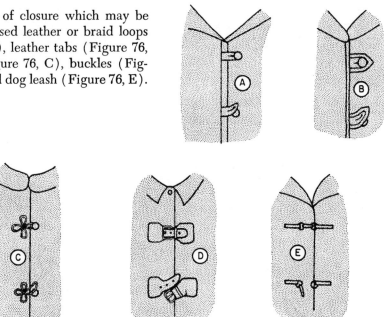

Figure 76

7

CARING FOR
LEATHER
AND SUEDE

PRESSING LEATHER

Pressing leather, unlike fabric, is accomplished not only by heat and the pressure of the iron, but also with rubber cement and the tapping pressure of a mallet. Pounding causes the seams to stay flat with less tension.

Equipment.

Iron.

Ironing board.

Glue: rubber cement with a brush or syringe for an applicator.

Mallet covered with leather.

Brown paper or press cloth.

Procedure.

Press seams, darts, and hems with the fabric dial set on the lowest setting (moderately warm). Use brown paper or a press cloth over the leather (Figure 77). *Do not use steam.* Leather can be pressed on either side if brown paper or a pressing cloth is placed between the leather and the iron. Exception: Cobraskins may be pressed with steam at a low temperature.

With colored suedes, cover the ironing board with brown paper because

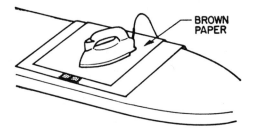

Figure 77

the suede color will crock, or rub off, on the ironing board cover.

Skive the raw edges to remove bulk. See p. 27.

Glue seams, hems, etc. Finger press into position. Pound gently with a leather-covered mallet. Allow to dry.

Lift up the seams and darts gently so that lines will not show on the right side.

NOTE: Top press all garments before and after linings are put in.

CARE OF LEATHER AND SUEDE GARMENTS AND ACCESSORIES

1. Never use wire brushes. They will scratch or cut the leather.
2. Be careful of salt spray on garments and boots; if left on, it discolors and stiffens leather and suede.
3. Imported glove kidskin is unfinished leather so it must never be touched by a liquid cleaner.
4. Since permanent softening is part of the process for capeskin suedes, do not use softeners; however, you may use them to restore old leather.
5. Avoid storing leather garments or gloves in tightly closed plastic bags. They are oxygen-proof and gradually a gas forms which discolors the leather. Plastic placed tightly around handbags sticks to them and destroys the finish.
6. Store leather garments in a roomy closet where they will not be crushed.
7. If leather garments are to be stored for some time, put them in a well-ventilated place at normal room temperature (65 to 70°)

with a relative humidity of approximately fifty percent. If the storage closet is too humid, mildew will form.

8. Do not spray moth-repellent solutions on leather. Chemical fumes discolor leather. On the other hand, suedes must be cleaned and treated with moth repellent before they are stored.
9. One should expect suedes to crock (the color rubs off), especially when it is new. Crocking is a natural result of sueding the leather. The fine particles of suede dust which rub off at first will gradually disappear. Rubbing with a towel will remove most of them.
10. Avoid extremes of light and heat for suedes of blue, green, and gray as a precaution against fading.
11. Rain will not harm the garment. Many smooth leathers are given a water-repellent finish at the tanner and need only to be wiped dry with a damp cloth. Allow leather to dry away from the heat, never near a radiator or other direct source of heat. It will cause the leather to stiffen.
12. Wear a scarf around your neck when wearing leather garments to avoid neckline soil.
13. Hang garments on padded hangers to prevent the shoulders from losing their shape.
14. If a garment needs pressing, use heavy brown paper or a press cloth between the iron and the leather. Set the iron at the lowest temperature and move it constantly to avoid overheating. *Never use steam.*
15. Combination leather and fabric garments should be cleaned professionally.

16. One need not cream or polish handbags very often. Too much wax and polish removes the tanner's finish and makes the surface gummy.

 a) Alligator, lizard, and snakeskin keep their patina indefinitely without any preparations.

 b) Sponge and brush suede, buckskin, and antelope to remove soil and to prevent the nap from matting.

 c) Clean patent leather with a mild solution of vinegar and water. Polish it with a touch of vaseline on a soft cloth.

GENERAL CLEANING OF LEATHER AND SUEDE

Cleaning leather garments, particularly suede, has become much less of a problem today than in past decades. Suede trim used to cause bleeding on garments and these dye stains were very difficult to remove. Today, suedes and leathers are readily cleaned by reputable cleaners familiar with handling leather garments. Many establishments today have spray equipment which adds oil to the leather when the original oil content has been reduced by repeated cleanings.

1. Dry clean leather garments at least once a year. Send it to a cleaner who specializes in handling leathers. Ordinary steam processes streak leather and destroy its color.

2. Do not let the garment become too heavily soiled before cleaning.

3. Inspect the garment carefully before cleaning. Look for stains and skin defects and point these out to the cleaners. Give the cleaners all of the information you have available from the hangtags. When buying leather or leather garments, always remember to save the hangtags. Use this information when caring for the garment yourself and pass it on to the dry cleaner.

4. All pieces of a matching ensemble should be cleaned and finished at the same time.

SPOT CLEANING

Spot clean leather garments as needed. Collars and cuffs may need to be cleaned often. Suede dust may be removed with cellophane tape, a dampened clothes brush, or terry cloth towel.

Suede.
Brush suede occasionally with a specially treated sponge usually included with the purchase of the garment. It removes suede dust and surface soil.

Spot cleaning solutions can be obtained from leather dealers (see "Suppliers for Miscellaneous Items," p. 65). Sewsoft Suede may be cleaned by brushing off soil with a slightly damp cloth. It is also washable with mild soap flakes. Bright colors may be expected to fade slightly just as corduroy does. Home spot removers may also be used if they are applied with a scrap of leather of the same color.

Most manufacturers do not recommend the use of dry cleaning solvents, shoe cleaning preparations or saddle soap for garment leathers. They tend to discolor the leather and leave ring marks.

A gum eraser, dry sponge, terry cloth towel, or soft-bristle brush are often recommended for spot removal.

A spray, *Suedeguard,* is available which

forms an invisible coating on the suede against dirt, spots, and stains.

A spray, *Spotlifter*, lifts oil or grease out of the suede.

Leathers.

Most smooth leathers can be cleaned with a damp sponge. It is often recommended that they be spot cleaned with a mild hand soap on a damp cloth. Rub gently and dry the leather with a soft, clean cloth.

Some manufacturers recommend that the leather be dusted with baking powder to seal the pores and then wiped with a dry cloth.

RUBBER CEMENT STAIN REMOVAL

Prepare a "Glue Ball."
1. Pour some rubber cement on a piece of glass and allow it to harden and dry.
2. Roll it into a ball.
3. Use the ball as an eraser to remove the excess rubber cement.

Dry Cleaning Solvents.

Benzine carbon tetrachloride, among others, may be used; however, they may affect color, so test them first.

8

MAKING A LEATHER OR SUEDE GARMENT

Full-length or ⅞-length coats and jackets may be made from leather as easily as from fabric. If the leather pieces are not large, select a design that lends itself to crosswise or lengthwise seams. In most cases, the procedure accompanying the pattern is satisfactory for use with leather. The few exceptions are listed below.

Procedure.
Select and plan a pattern to fit the leather pelts. See pp. 9–11, 16–17.

Make a muslin or fabric pattern.

1. Fit it to your complete satisfaction.
2. Transfer all necessary alterations to the paper pattern.

Lay out the pattern on the leather. See pp. 17–20.

Cut out the leather garment. See p. 20.

Mark the leather. See p. 21.

Cut and construct the interfacing for the garment front.

1. Cut the front interfacing so that it is 1 inch wider than the inner edge of the facing and extends to the armhole (Figure 78, A). The extra interfacing is cut for better shape retention.
2. Trim the seam allowance (⅜ inch) + ⅛ inch at the coat front. Stitch ⅜ inch linen tape to the front edge, extending it ⅛ inch beyond the trimmed edge of the interfacing (Figure 78, B).
3. For raglan sleeves, cut the interfacing to the seam (Figure 79, A).
4. For kimono sleeves, extend the interfacing to the shoulder and design

an imaginary armhole line (Figure 79, B).

Construct the darts. See p. 31.

Baste the front and back seams together with mending tape before stitching. See "Basting," p. 24; "Seams," pp. 25–31.

Construct the pockets and other fashion details.

1. Place a fabric stay on the wrong side of the leather under the pocket mouth line.
2. Welts and flaps may have interfacings of lightweight canvas or pellon glued or stitched in the seams.
3. Narrow linen tape glued at the fold lines of welts or attached to the interfacings prevents them from stretching. Tape may also be used at the top of patch pockets.

Glue the interfacing to the garment front. (Release the interfacing from the garment later, as the neck, front and side seams will be caught in the seam allowance.)

Make bound buttonholes if the garment calls for them. See p. 34.

Attach the front facing to the garment, catching the edge of the linen tape which is stitched onto the interfacing. Press the facing, turn it and remove the bulk. Grade the seams (see pp. 26–27). Anchor the facing seams with rubber cement.

Baste and sew the side and shoulder seams, using linen tape in the seams to keep them from stretching. See p. 25.

Prepare and set the collar.

1. Interface the collar with lightweight canvas, bias pellon, organdy, or stiffened lawn. Choose the interfacing which is most appropriate for

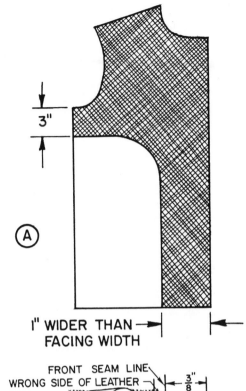

I" WIDER THAN FACING WIDTH

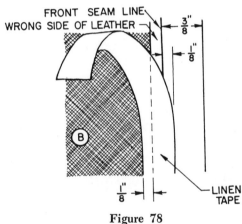

FRONT SEAM LINE
WRONG SIDE OF LEATHER

LINEN TAPE

Figure 78

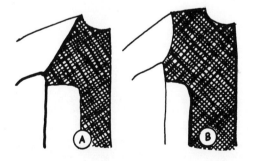

Figure 79

the weight of the leather. See "Interfacings," p. 15.

2. The top collar should be cut a little larger than the undercollar.
3. Grade the seams and remove all excess bulk before turning. See pp. 26–27.
4. Press and glue the seams.
5. Apply the collar as directed in the pattern instructions.

Set in the sleeves. Glue them to check the fit. Since leather adapts itself to the wearer and folds tend to form, allow some additional sleeve length.

Hem the garment with rubber cement.

Release the "glued" interfacings. See p. 33.

Top press the complete garment. See p. 46.

Line the garment.

1. Machine stitch the lining pieces together. The sleeve linings may be sewn in by hand. Attach the lining by hand at the bottom of the sleeves and garment if free lining is not desired. Coat lining hems are usually free and jacket linings are usually attached.
2. Method One: seam or bias tape.
    a) Stitch matching seam or bias tape to the facing edges.
    b) Hand stitch the lining to the tape, using the slip stitch (Figure 80).

c) Hand or machine stitch the lining hem.
d) The lining is easily removable for dry cleaning or laundering.

3. Method Two: bias binding, cording, or braid.
    a) Cut a bias binding strip 2 inches wide and fold it in half. Cording or braid may be used as an alternative.
    b) Stitch the bias binding to the facing of the garment, placing the binding edges even with the leather edges (Figure 81).
    c) Hand stitch the lining to the bias binding.
4. Method Three: snap tape.
    a) Machine stitch the socket side of the snap tape to the facing (Figure 82).
    b) Fold the lining edge under and stitch the ball side of the snap tape to the edge of the lining (Figure 83).
    c) Machine or hand stitch the lining hem free from the garment.
    d) This is an ideal method for a snap-in fur or quilted lining for winter and twill lining for warmer weather.
5. Method Four: zip-in lining.
    a) Attach the zipper to the coat facing. The lining usually zips from right to left.
        i) Bind the inside of the coat facing with a matching bias tape.

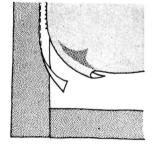

Figure 80

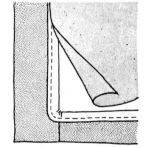

Figure 81

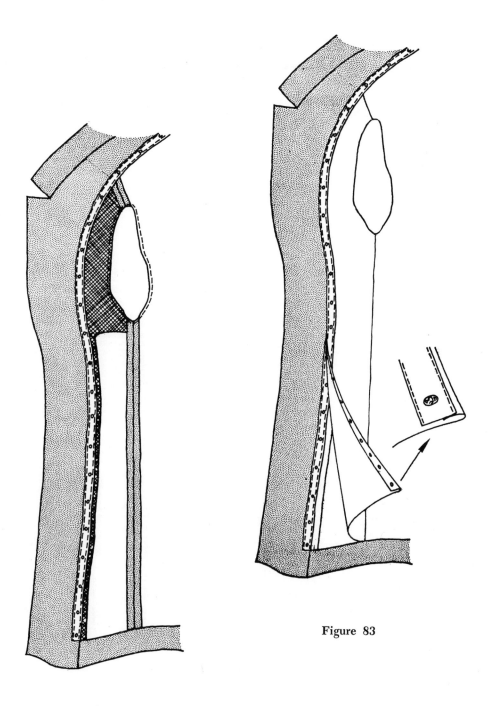

Figure 82

Figure 83

ii) Match the center marking of a separating zipper to the center back neck facing with the zipper face up.

iii) Place the bound edge of the facing on top of the zipper, extending the edge about ¼ inch beyond the zipper teeth (Figure 84). Using a zipper foot, stitch the inner edge of the zipper tape to the facing. Stitch only through the tape and the facing.

b) Complete the lining.

i) Fit the lining to the coat, pinning the lining to the coat at the armscye edges (the armscye is the hole in the garment into which the arm is fitted) and the side seams.

ii) Lap the front and neck edges of the lining over the free edge of the zipper tape. Turn under the excess lining and clip the zipper tape so it fits the curve smoothly.

c) Attach the lining to the zipper.

i) Separate the zipper.

ii) Using a zipper foot, stitch the lining to the zipper tape for the entire length of the zipper (Figure 85).

d) Complete the zip-out lining.

i) Sew snaps at the armhole and the side seams to connect the lining and coat at the shoulder.

ii) Snaps or loops and buttons may be sewn at the bottom of the sleeve edge to connect the sleeve lining to the coat.

iii) Hem the lining about 1 inch shorter than the coat.

Top press the garment. (NOTE: Mink "wedding ring" collars may be attached to a collarless leather garment. See p. 134.)

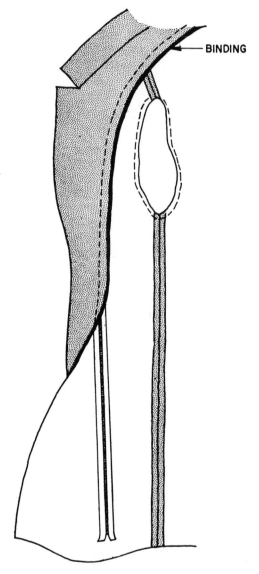

BINDING

Figure 84

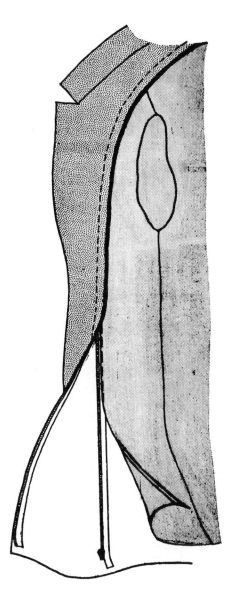

Figure 85

LEATHER SKIRTS, SHORTS, AND SLACKS

Procedure.
Select a design with simple lines and few seams. An additional front or back seam may be added to facilitate laying out the pattern. Gored skirts or A-line designs are good choices for leather.

Make a muslin pattern and fit it. Transfer the alterations to the paper pattern. Remember that stitch marks show, so proceed with care.

Lay out the pattern. Cut and mark it as suggested on pp. 17–21.

Complete the darts and skirt seams. See pp. 22–32.

Put in the zipper or nylon closure and press the skirt. See pp. 38–42.

Prepare the lining. Stitch the lining together except for the waistband and the placket opening. Press the lining.

Preparing and attaching the waistband.

1. Method One: all-leather waistband for lightweight smooth leather.
   a) Cut the belt twice the desired finished width plus two seam allowances. For the length, add 2½ inches to the waist measurement to allow for the seams.
   b) Press the waistband in half lengthwise.
   c) Cut canvas interfacing the full length, but only half the width, of the belt.
   d) Stitch the interfacing ⅛ to ¼ inch below the fold line on the inside of the band (Figure 86).

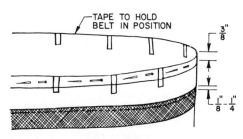

Figure 86

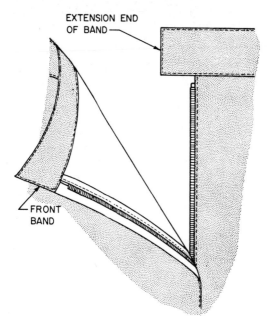

EXTENSION END OF BAND

FRONT BAND

Figure 87

FRONT BAND

EXTENSION

Figure 88

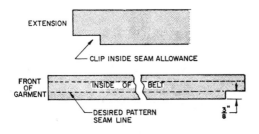

EXTENSION

CLIP INSIDE SEAM ALLOWANCE

FRONT OF GARMENT

INSIDE OF BELT

DESIRED PATTERN SEAM LINE

Figure 89

e) Close the ends of the waistband. The extension may be from the back for a nylon tape and large hook closure or from the front for a button and buttonhole closure (Figure 87).

i) Stitch the ends of the belt with the right sides together in a ⅜ inch seam.

ii) Continue stitching along the edge of the band which extends beyond the skirt (Figure 88).

iii) Trim the interfacing close to the line of stitching on the ends of the waistband (Figure 88).

iv) Trim, grade, and skive the seam allowances at the corners of the band ends. Turn the band right side out.

v) Clip the seam allowance on the inside of the band (Figure 89).

f) Attach the band to the skirt.

i) Place the lining inside the skirt with the seams toward the skirt seams. Tape it into position.

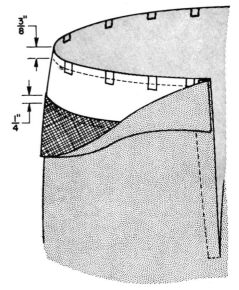

Figure 90

ii) Place the right side of the front band against the right side of the skirt. One side of the belt should be even with the zipper placket and the end of the extension stitching should be even with the placket on the other side (Figure 90). Ease the skirt top onto the band. Hold it in place with mending tape.

iii) Stitch ⅜ inch seam and press the band into position.

iv) Turn down the underside of the band. Do not turn it under. Baste the band with mending tape.

v) Turn the skirt to the right side. Stitch by machine through all thicknesses around the waistline in the seam-line groove (Figure 91).

vi) Trim back the interfacing to the line of stitching.

2. Method Two: waistband faced with grosgrain ribbon for suede skirts.

a) Cut the waistband the desired

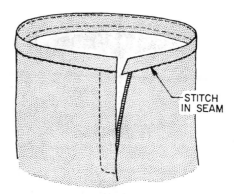

Figure 91

width plus two seam allowances. The length is equal to the waist measurement plus 2¼ inches (Figure 92, A).

b) Glue canvas interfacing in the belt inside the seam allowances (Figure 92, B).

c) Fold down the top seam allowance. Stitch the grosgrain ribbon to the fold of the band's top seam allowance (Figure 92, C).

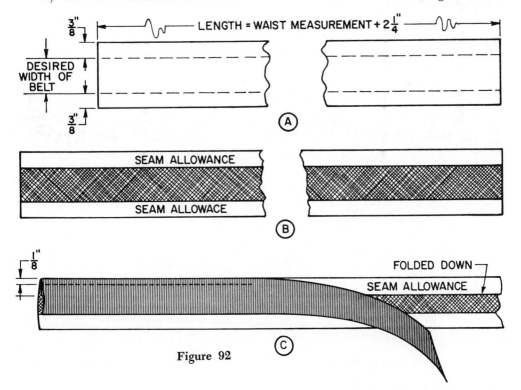

Figure 92

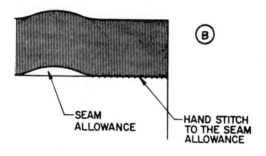

MAGIC MENDING TAPE TO HOLD
BELT IN POSITION FOR STITCHING

STITCH ALONG SEAM
ALLOWANCE LINE

MAGIC MENDING
TAPE TO HOLD
LINING TO LEATHER

Ⓐ

Figure 93

Ⓑ

SEAM
ALLOWANCE

HAND STITCH
TO THE SEAM
ALLOWANCE

d) Close the ends of the band. See Method One, p. 56, 1e.

e) Place the lining inside the skirt with the seams toward the skirt seams and tape it into position.

OPTIONAL: The lining may be machine-stitched ⅛ inch from the edge (Figure 92, C).

f) Attach the band.

i) Place the right side of the lower seam of the band against the right side of the top of the skirt (Figure 93, A).

ii) Stitch a ⅜ inch seam and remove the tape.

iii) Press the band up.

iv) Attach the bottom of the grosgrain ribbon by hand to the seam allowance which has been folded under (Figure 93, B).

NOTE: If you topstitch around the entire band, omit Step A above.

3. Method Three: on heavier leather skirts, omit the waistband.

a) Stitch the lining and the skirt top together, wrong sides together, about ¼ inch from the edge (Figure 94).

b) Fold back the skirt lining ⅜ inch to the inside and topstitch

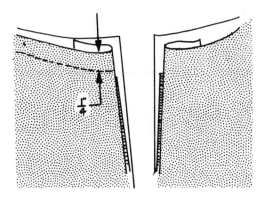

Figure 94

the belting to the top of the skirt. The wrong side of the belting should be toward the skirt lining about ⅛ inch from the folded edge (Figure 95).

c) The lower edge of the belting is left free and may be tacked by hand at the ends and at the seam lines.

To complete the skirt, turn the raw edges of the lining around the placket and sew them by hand to the zipper tape or to the seam if another type of closure is used.

Glue or self-stitch the hem into position. See p. 33. The lining hem is self-stitched and hemmed about 1 inch shorter than the skirt.

VESTS AND WESKITS

Procedure.

After choosing the pattern, cut and fit a muslin garment. Transfer alterations to the printed pattern before cutting the leather (pp. 16–21).

Line the leather garment completely.

Omit all facings on weskits and vests and line the garment to the edge. Grosgrain ribbon may be attached on the inside for reinforcement of front or back openings (Figure 96). Omit zippers if the garment will slide over the head easily.

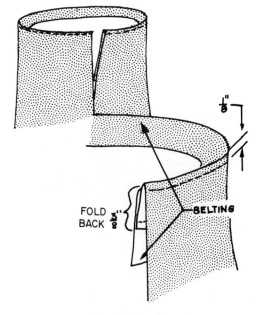

Figure 95

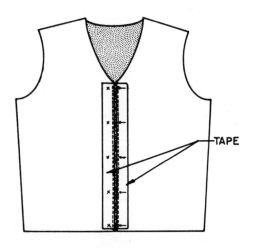

Figure 96

Glue interfacing to the leather around the neck, the armholes, and in front openings (Figure 97).

Topstitching by hand or machine around the neck, front, and hem edges holds the lining in position. If topstitching is not desired, gluing the leather seam back also keeps the lining from showing. Be careful not to get the glue on the lining because it stains.

Buttonholes may be bound, machine made, or handworked.

Vests, boleros, or weskits which open in the front or back.

1. Join the shoulder seams of the lining and the leather separately and press them open. (See pp. 23–29.)
2. Put the lining on the leather, right sides together.
3. Stitch the armholes and the front neckline openings (Figure 98). Trim, grade, and skive the seams. (See pp. 26–27.)
4. Turn the vest right side out by pulling the lining through the shoulder tunnels, and press it.
5. Join the lining seams from the hem to the armhole (Figure 99).
6. Join the garment seams from the hem to the armhole (Figure 100).
7. Repeat fifth and sixth steps under "Procedure" on the other side seam.
8. Glue the leather hem. The lining hem may be hemmed separately or attached to the leather.

Pullover vests.

1. Join the side seams of the garment and the lining separately and press them open (Figure 100). (See pp. 23–29.)

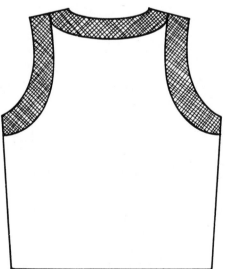

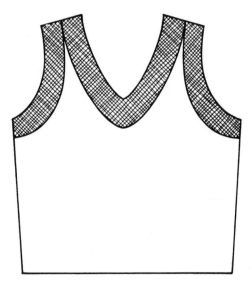

Figure 97

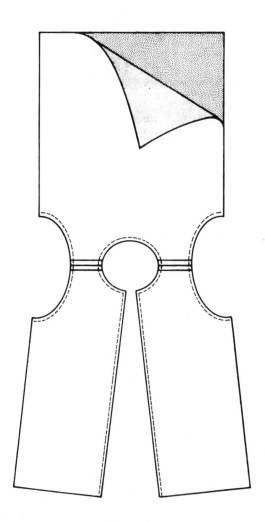

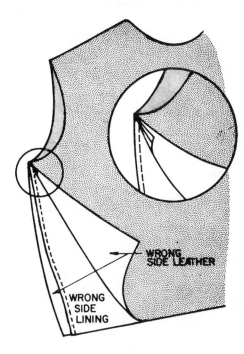

Figure 99

Figure 98

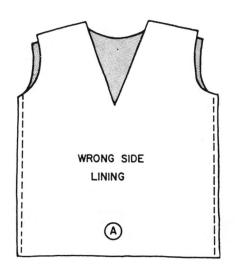

WRONG SIDE
LINING

(A)

WRONG SIDE
LEATHER

(B)

Figure 100

Figure 101

WRONG SIDE LINING

WRONG SIDE LEATHER

WRONG SIDE LEATHER

WRONG SIDE LINING

Figure 102

2. Join the lining to the leather at the armhole and the neckline (Figure 101). The lining shoulder seams are turned back on the seam allowance toward the wrong side. Clip, grade, and skive the seams. Turn and press them.

3. Sew the leather shoulder seams and press them.

4. Tuck the leather shoulder seam under the lining and close the lining shoulder seams by hand (Figure 102).

5. Complete hem as explained for vests and boleros above. (See also p. 33.)

CONSTRUCTION TIPS FOR VARIOUS PROJECTS

Elbow patches may be purchased already cut or cut from scrap leather. They may be attached by machine or by hand with a running or uneven backstitch. Leather *binding* or *piping* may be purchased by the yard or cut from scrap leather. Apply it to straight or only slightly curved edges because leather is difficult to ease into a curved edge. To apply binding or piping, stitch the right side of the binding against the right side of the garment. Turn the binding to the wrong side, but do not turn it under. Stitch from the right side in the seam groove to attach the binding on the inside. *Flowers* and *leaves* for hat trim may be cut and sewed as fabric flowers. Leather may be carved for leaf veins and other fashion details. Leather or suede may be combined attractively with fabrics or knits for jackets, coats, and walking suits using the leather for yokes, garment fronts, or the entire body of a garment. Front facing trim and pocket welts of leather are other possibilities. *Wool braid or bias strips* of wool or satin may be used to bind raw edges of leather or suede garments. *Bags, belts,* and *gloves* may be made from scrap leather. Bag frames and belt kits are helpful in creating these accessories.

GLOSSARY OF LEATHER AND SUEDE TERMS

Back. A side with the belly cut off.

Bevel. Reducing the thickness of leather by removing a portion of it at an angle from the cut edge.

Corrected grain. Leather which has been lightly sanded on the grain side.

Crock. The tendency for color to rub off new leather, particularly new suedes.

Embossing. A finishing design put on skins by a heavy plating machine; for example, pigskin texture embossed on sheepskin.

Full grain. Leather which has been tanned and finished without disturbing the grain by buffing or sandpapering.

Glaze. A spray applied to leather which gives a high, glossy finish.

Grain. The outermost layer of the animal's skin; it is often a distinctive pattern after the hair has been removed.

Hides. Leather from larger animals which weigh 25 pounds or more.

Kips. Leather from animals that weigh from 15 to 25 pounds.

Patina. (1) A process for softening leather; (2) an external design which is artificially applied.

Plated. Ironed.

Shaving. A process of removing a portion of the leather with abrasive paper attached to a large revolving cylinder.

Shaving dust. Dust accumulated on the back of skins after splitting and shaving them. It is removed by rubbing with a cloth dampened in a vinegar and water solution (one part vinegar to two parts water).

Side. One half of a skin or hide.

Skins. (1) Leather tanned in the whole pelt, the same size and shape as the animal; (2) the covering of smaller animals such as calves, sheep, and goats.

Skiving. Reducing the thickness of leather by shaving it on the wrong side.

Splits. The flesh or bottom layer of a hide which has been cut in half.

Splitting. A process of removing a portion of the leather with a circular knife revolving between two pulleys so that there will be two layers of useable leather. Splitting is used on heavier skins such as deer and pig.

Staking. Washing leather over metal stakes to break the exterior crust formed during tanning.

Synthetic leather. Cloth which is coated with vinyl and is finished or embossed to resemble a variety of leathers. It is sold by the yard.

Tanning. The process by which animal skins and hides are transformed into soft, flexible leather by treating them with chemicals and bark extracts.

Chrome tanning. Tanning with the use of chemicals to make leather water resistant.

Vegetable tanning. Tanning with the use of extracts from tree barks.

Toggling. Stretching leather to remove excess elasticity.

Top grain. The grain layer of a split skin or hide.

BOOKS AND BULLETINS

Bouquet, Gus. *The Techniques of Making Leather Garments.* Fort Worth, Texas: The Tandy Leather Company, 1959.

Hummel, Edith M. *You Can Make Your Own Bags and Accessories.* New York: Fairchild Publications, Inc., 1952; Reprint, 1957.

Landry, Lenore. *Using Today's Fabrics.* Circular 630, Madison, Wisconsin; The University of Wisconsin, Extension Service, College of Agriculture, May, 1964.

Petersen, Grete. *Creative Leather.* New York: Sterling Publishing Co., Inc., 1960.

———. *Leather in Our Lives.* New York: Leather Industries of America, 411 Fifth Ave., New York, New York 10016.

———. *Sewing with Leather.* Fort Worth, Texas: The Tandy Leather Company, 1959.

———. *Leathers in Fashion.* New York, New York: McCall's Patterns' Fabric Information.

LEATHER SUPPLIERS

Many department stores across the nation carry suede and leather skins in the yard goods department. Other suppliers are listed below:

Creative Leather Workshop
Box 1495
Prudential Central Station
Boston, Massachusetts 02199
Lambskin suede, buckskin and lambskin grain leather.

J. P. Fliegel Co.
P.O. Box 505
Gloversville, New York
Cape, deerskin, peccary, suede, Pigtex, lambskin, and glove leather. Samples on request.

Franken Trimming & Co., Inc.
1400 Broadway
New York, New York
Suede, leather and cobra bandings, and cording.

A. L. Gebhardt Co.
226 N. Water Street
Milwaukee, Wisconsin 53202
Brown, beige, and white garment leather (capeskin).

Janice Leather, Ltd.
30 West 24th Street
New York, New York 10010
Sheer suedes available in many colors, also leathers and cobraskins. Available in many retail yard good departments of department stores and fabric houses.

Willard Helburn, Inc.
22 Wallis Street
Peabody, Massachusetts
Sewsoft sheer suede in twelve colors.

Laurence and Klauber
1412 Broadway
New York, New York

Walter Loeber Co.
3108 W. Meinecke Avenue
Milwaukee, Wisconsin 53208
Hair calf, cabretta, deerskins, suedes, and sheepskin. Wholesale and retail.

Lowenthal Trimming Corp.
140 West 31st Street
New York, New York

Sax-Crafts
1101 N. 3rd Street
Milwaukee, Wisconsin 53203
Capeskin and suedes.

Sills & Co.
48 West 37th Street
New York, New York 10018
Suedes and leathers in many colors.

Tandy Leather Company
P.O. Box 791
Fort Worth, Texas
(105 nationwide stores)
Garment suede, Plainsman sheer suede, snow white shelter cape, Princess garment lamb, cabretta, glove horse, and short-hair calf. Catalog available.

Tiedemann Leather Co.
2252 Elston Avenue
Chicago, Illinois 60614

SUPPLIERS FOR MISCELLANEOUS ITEMS

Deerskin Trading Post
Rt. 1 114B
Danvers, Mass. 01923
Persuede (color, erasing action).
Suedeguard (spray to form invisible coating against dirt, spots, stains).
Spot-Lifter (spray lifts oil, grease).

J. & J. Sewing Supplies
5506 Goucher Lane
Monona, Wisconsin 53716
Interfacings, subsilk thread, zip-in lining zippers, glover's needles, sewing machine needles, linen tape for seams, beeswax, wax crayon, linings, etc.

Janice Leathers, Inc.
30 West 24th Street
New York, New York 10010
  Persuede to clean suede (available in colors).

Leathercraft Products Corp.
54 West 56th St.
New York, N. Y. 10019
  Suede-Crafter to clean suede; *Leather-crafter* to clean leather. (Spray.)

Pursenalities
1619 Grand Avenue
Baldwin, New York
  Purse frames.

Singer Sewing Co.
  Singer Leather Point Needles (15 x 2) (assortment of three machine needles with wedge points).

Tandy Leather Co.
P.O. Box 791
Fort Worth, Texas
(105 nationwide stores)
  Rubber cement and glue, mallets, skivers, punch pliers, elbow patches, glover's needles, etc., *Persuede* for cleaning suede.

Unique Zipper Co.
P.O. Box 2255
Main Office Station
Seattle, Washington 98111
  Unique invisible zipper and zipper foot.

Velma's Sewing & Specialty Shop
Route 1 Box 166
McFarland, Wisconsin
  Covering of leather and fur buttons.

LEATHER CLEANERS AND TANNERS

If you are unable to locate a reputable dry cleaner for the cleaning of leather garments in your area, you may mail your garment to one of the addresses listed below:

Adelman Laundry and Dry Cleaners
709 E. Capitol Drive
Milwaukee, Wisconsin 53212
  Leather and suede refinishing department.

Glove Masters
451 East 167th Street, Dept. DM
Bronx, New York 10456
  Specialists in suede and leather cleaning. Price list upon request.

Guaranteed Suede Cleaners
Salem, Massachusetts
  Clean suedes. Price list upon request.

Kleen-All Leather Co.
P.O. Box 7267
Milwaukee, Wisconsin 53213
  Suede and leather cleaning, retint, refinish, wholesale and retail.

Leathercraft Process of America Inc.
54 W. 56th St.
New York, N. Y. 10019
  Clean suedes and leathers, alter, repair, restore color, texture and oils, and replace buttons.

Suedecare-Leathercare
54 Station Plaza
Hempstead, New York
  Cleaning and refinishing suede and leather. Price list upon request.

TANNERS FOR DEERSKIN HIDES

See p. 5 for care of hides in preparation for tanning.

Custom Coat Company, Inc.
227 N. Washington Street
Berlin, Wisconsin
  Tan hides, dye hides, make leather garments, gloves, moccasins, handbags, and accessories. Catalog available.

W. B. Place & Company
Hartford, Wisconsin
  Tans and tailors deerskins into garments, gloves, moccasins, purses, etc. Catalog available.

DRAWING KEY

LEATHER—RIGHT SIDE		FUR SIDE
LEATHER—WRONG SIDE		SKIN SIDE
LINING—RIGHT SIDE		GROSGRAIN
LINING—WRONG SIDE		TWILL TAPE
INTERFACING		UNDERLINING

The various drawings indicate the characteristics of the materials to be used. By comparing the shadings in the drawings throughout the book with this key, you will be able to select the appropriate material for the job.

FUR

Vogue Pattern #7515

1

FUR—THEN
AND NOW

Among early man's basic needs in cold climates was warm clothing. Historians consider it a reasonable conjecture that soon after man learned to use animals for food, he discovered the use of their skins for clothing.

Primitive man obtained skins from the animals he could most easily slay with his rudimentary weapons. Bear and reindeer were the most common game. The skins were dried and cured, and softened for wear by beating them with a stick. They were draped around the body so that the right arm was free.

One of the early types of garments sewn from fur skins was the Mongolian Cross. It was formed in a broad cross shape with a large hole cut in the center for the head. Two ends were sewn together to form short sleeves while the other two ends were sewn together to complete the body.

Although fur was a necessity in the North, it was a luxury in more temperate climates. Furs were highly valued in China and Japan as early as 1500 B.C. An indication of fur's appeal to women is the report that Semiramis, Queen of Assyria in 800 B.C., brought back eight thousand tiger skins from India. Ancient Egyptian drawings portray the use of fur among the royalty for decorative household trappings such as upholstery for stools. In Egyptian state ceremonials, whole skins were draped over the shoulders with the paws tied across the chest.

With the increase in sea commerce, the uses of fur expanded throughout the whole of ancient civilization. Fur was always a mark of the upper classes and by the time of the Middle Ages had become a status symbol. It was worn at all times and in as large a quantity as the season would permit. In very cold weather, fur garments were worn one over the other. During the thirteenth century, the demand for fur was so great that those who could not afford expensive furs wore skins of lamb, rabbit, dogs, and cats. Because of the shortages that were developing and also from a desire to retain fur as a mark of status for the upper classes, France and England enacted laws prohibiting commoners from owning more expensive furs.

Shortly after the discovery of the American continents, Europeans learned of the limitless supply of fur in North America. Fur pelts, especially beaver skins, were used as money in trade. With the discovery of the new supply, fur was used even more extensively than it had been previously. Among others, the use of the tippet came into vogue. The tippet was a single pelt, with jewel-encrusted nose and paws, which dangled from a waist chain or from one shoulder. Men's furs also became more ostentatious. Fur cuffs and collar trim became larger. Men also adopted the use of the woman's muff; the muff increased so greatly in size that by the end of the eighteenth century, the largest of them scarcely fit under one's arm.

Toward the end of the eighteenth century, the popularity of stylized fur pieces for women is noted. It was not until the twentieth century, however, that fur was worn extensively on outside garments. Fur was used for trim and lining until the middle of the nineteenth century when it was tentatively introduced as an outer garment in France. The first ladies' stylized fur garments were fashioned from black-dyed Alaskan seal. In the twentieth century, mink, sable, muskrat, squirrel, and Persian lamb have been brought into the fashion scene.

The United States pioneered the development of ranch bred mutation mink. Fur is now a $350,000,000 industry in the United States and mink accounts for approximately eighty-five percent of this total. Using the latest scientific breeding practices known, the mink rancher has been able to produce twenty-two shades of natural colored fur.

2

SELECTING FURS AND PATTERNS

FURS

There are two sources of fur open to the home sewer. First, new pelts are available at fur supply houses and ranches throughout the country (see p. 143). Second, used fur coats may be completely dismantled and restyled according to the latest vogue.

The selection of new fur will not be treated at length in this book. For complete information, it is suggested that you consult one of the specialized books listed on p. 143.

Used fur is available in many different ways. Perhaps you have an outdated fur coat which shows some signs of wear, but is still in good condition, generally speaking. Many secondhand stores have good used coats from which up-to-date garments can be made. Closets of friends and relatives may also produce used garments for restyling. Some retail furriers are willing to sell used fur garments.

An important factor to keep in mind in selecting used fur is that only a garment smaller than the original can be made from it. After a garment is disassembled, pockets sewn together, and worn areas replaced, there is less useable fur. However, it is also possible to use two furs which are identical or compatible. Good combinations are mink and seal, mink and Persian lamb, or Persian lamb and seal.

It is advisable to check the skin for dryness and brittleness. The skin may have been dried out due to improper storage. Open the lining of the used garment along the hemline. If the leather gives way when slightly pulled or if it tears easily, it may not be worth restyling. If the fur is in good condition and there is an adequate supply, you will be able to make a garment which is as chic today as it was originally.

PATTERNS

Patterns can be obtained from fur supply houses (see p. 143) or simple-lined dressmaker patterns. These patterns should have basic lines similar to those shown in Figures 1 and 2. Some hints in selecting a dressmaker pattern are given below.

Figure 1

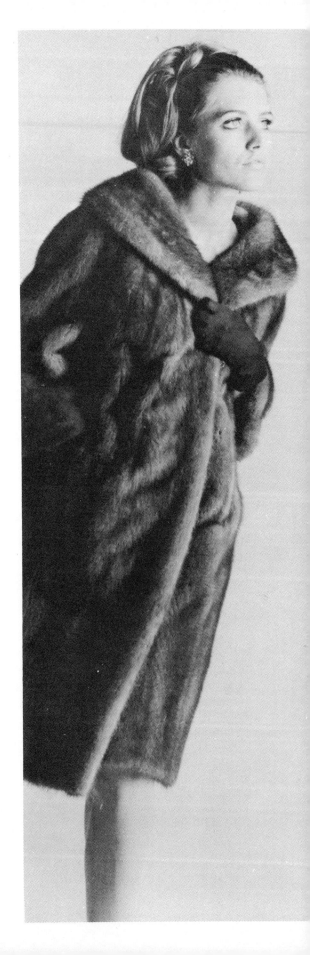

Figure 2

Figure 3

Coat patterns with set-in sleeves may be used; however, raglan and modified raglan sleeves are highly recommended. In addition to ease of construction, there is less strain on the fur. Select a dressmaker pattern for the neckline and sleeve which comes closest to the style desired for the fur garment. Do not alter the neckline of a pattern. Shawl, convertible, or wedding-ring collars may be made.

A full-length coat pattern can be shortened to make a short jacket, car coat, or ¾- to ⅞-length coat. The sleeve length may be varied. Cuffs and bands are recommended to give additional sleeve length.

The following alterations are suggested when using a dressmaker pattern:

1. Eliminate buttons and buttonholes except for fashion purposes. Plan to fasten the garment with hooks and ·eyes.
2. Eliminate patch pockets and use set-in pockets.
3. Eliminate the outer sleeve seam in a raglan sleeve by laying the two sleeve pattern sections together and treating them as one piece. A dart is formed at the shoulder.
4. Eliminate any pattern lines which are unnecessary to the general shape of the garment.
5. Eliminate the center back seam if possible. A back seam may be necessary because of the location of worn areas in the fur.

After a pattern is selected, construct a practice garment from an old sheet or unbleached muslin. After fitting the cloth, transfer all of the necessary alterations to the paper pattern. *Remove all of the seam allowances on the pattern before laying it on the fur.*

When checking the cloth pattern, it is important to note the following points:

1. Bustline darts should end 1 in. from the tip of the bust.
2. When using a raglan sleeve, the length and depth of the dart will depend upon the slope of the shoulder.
3. Both the sleeve length and the garment length depend upon the amount of fur and the height and weight of the wearer. Jackets and stoles should end above the largest measurement of the hip, *not* at the hipline.

3

EQUIPMENT
AND
SUPPLIES

The materials used to restyle a fur garment are very few in number and easily obtainable. The notion counter of a department or hardware store can supply most of them. A furrier's supply company will have any other equipment difficult to obtain.

EQUIPMENT

Ball-point pen. Used for marking the skin side of the fur and to make notations on the muslin.

Brads. No. 18 or finer. Used to nail out large pieces of fur (Figure 4).

Cardboard strips and pieces. Lightweight cardboard similar to cereal boxes and tablet backs. Strips are ½ in. by 12 to 18 in. Pieces are approximately 8 by 12 in.

Clip, hair. A metal 4 in. hair clip (Figure 5) used to hold in place the folded edges of the boa after shaping.

Cutting tools.
  Razor blades, single edge (Figure 6).
  Furrier's knife made from a single section of steel or a holder with one half a double-edge razor blade (Figure 7).

Felt pen. Black or dark brown, depending upon the color of the hair. Used to touch up small areas of off-color fur.

Glass-head pins. Two-in. pins used to pin the pattern to the skin. They are also used to mark specific areas of fur for replacement or the line of stripe (Figure 8).

Hammer. A hammer with a small head, such as a tack hammer, used to pound brads into the nailing board.

Ice pick. Used to make a hole in a pelt's rubber skull for the shank of the glass eye.

Nailing board. A flat, wooden surface on which fur is nailed. The surface may be one of the following: a 4 by 8 ft. piece of plywood, an attic floor, the reverse side of a ping-pong table, or several pieces of wood butted together. A softwood nailing board is desirable for nailing out collars, boas, and fashion detail pieces.

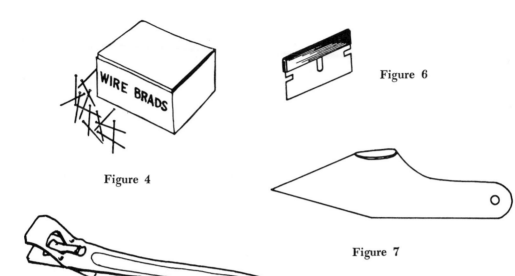

Figure 4

Figure 6

Figure 7

Figure 5

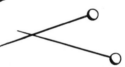

Needles.

Glover's Needle. A three-sided needle which cuts a small triangular hole in the skin so that the thread glides rather than drags when pulled (Figure 9). It is used to sew through two thicknesses of skin. The needles range in size from No. 3 to 8. The larger the size number, the finer the needle. The size of the needle depends on the thickness and toughness of the skin. It should be as small as possible.

Sharps. A needle which is round in cross section and is used to sew the folded edges of the lining over the permanently basted sewing edge. It may be used to sew two extremely tender thicknesses of skin together. The size range is from No. 1 to 12.

Pinch clip. Used to shape faces on mink skins for neck scarves (Figure 10).

Push pins. A millinery or bulletin board pin used to nail fur on a nailing board (Figure 11).

Pliers. Used to remove brads from the nailing board.

Rubber or plastic gloves. Used to protect hands from stain when dyeing fur.

Ruler. It is desirable to have both a 12 to 15 in. straightedge and a yardstick.

Figure 8

Figure 9

Figure 10

Figure 11
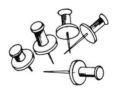

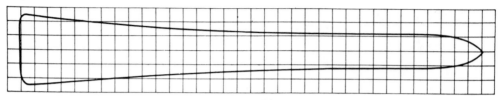

Figure 12

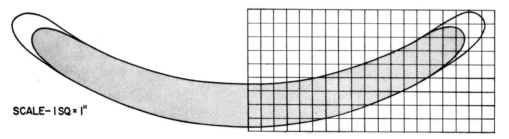

SCALE- I SQ = I"

Figure 13

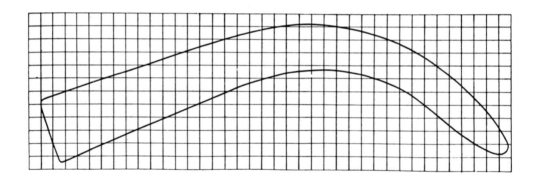

Figure 14

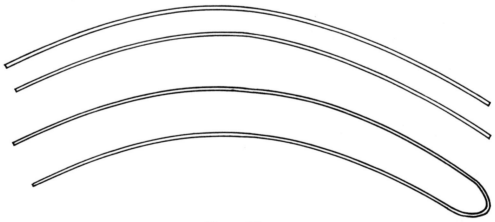

Figure 15

Shaped nailing boards. Designed to put a shape or curve into a mink skin. Basswood is generally used because it is soft and push pins are easily forced into it. Three kinds of nailing boards are shown in Figures 12 to 15.

Shaped wires. From straight lengths of steel, desired forms are made for shaping mink skins into boas and scarves (Figure 15). Use 3/16 in. cold-rolled steel, which is available in 12 ft. lengths from a hardware supply company. Each shape requires 6 ft. of steel. Since steel rusts, avoid letting it touch the hair side of the pelt. To prevent rusting, wrap the wire with transparent tape.

Shears. Used for cutting lining, interlining, and tapes. The handle is used for flattening seams.

Soap crayon. A wax crayon used to mark the skin side of the fur. It is used interchangeably with a ball-point pen (Figure 16).

Stapler. Either a paper or wood stapler which will force staples into wood. The tote size stapler is sufficient to nail mink onto a softwood nailing board. Staples 5/16 in. in length may be used to nail heavier pelts to a plywood nailing board.

Sponge. A small household sponge used to apply water and leather conditioner to the skin side of the fur.

Thimble. A metal or plastic cover for the third finger of the right hand.

Water container. A glass quart jar for mixing the concentrated leather conditioner with water.

Vegetable brush. A long-handled vegetable fiber brush to apply dye to fur.

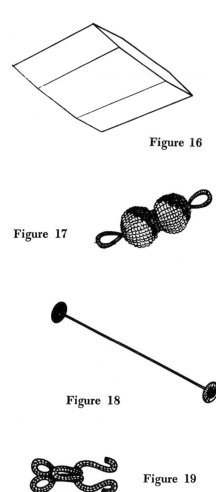

Figure 16

Figure 17

Figure 18

Figure 19

Figure 20

SUPPLIES

Cold tape. A tape which is adhesive on one side and silky on the other. It is used for staying edges.

Dye. A compounded dye for fur which gives it luster. It is available as an aerosol spray or liquid in various colors.

Findings.
> *Ball snaps.* Crochet-covered balls with snap ends used as fasteners on neck scarves (Figure 17).

Eyes. Glass eyes, plain or veined, used in the faces of neck scarf pelts (Figure 18). They are available in brown, blue, or natural colors.

Crocheted hooks, eyes, and rings. Made of strong steel and covered with thread in black, brown, grey, beige, and white (Figures 19, 20). Rings may be sewed together to form a chain for connecting ball snaps and fur in a neckpiece.

Figure 21

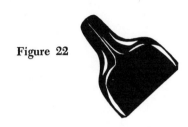

Figure 22

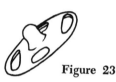

Figure 23

Figure 24

Figure 25

Jaw snaps. A steel spring with a crocheted covering over one of the arms (Figure 21). It is used in the head of the pelt to join the ends of a neck scarf or to fasten the ends of a boa together or to a garment. They are available in various colors to match the fur.

Skull. Premolded shapes, rubber or cork, inserted in the head of a pelt to give it shape (Figure 22).

Snaps. Large snaps, No. 4, covered with fabric (Figure 23). The fabric covering is fine and firm and matches the color of the fur.

Grosgrain ribbon. ⅝ in. width ribbon is used on the lower edge of jackets, stoles, and coats. One-inch width ribbon is used for pocket facings.

Interfacing. Feltlike material, sometimes called furrier's felt or fleece, which is placed between the front facing and the garment. It is also used in collars and cuffs. When furrier's felt is not available, high quality outing flannel may be used. Interfacing gives body to the front, collar, and cuffs.

Interfilling. Synthetic or wool wadding used to fill the mink skin used in a neck scarf. It is also used to fill the area between the skin and ribbon in a boa. Wool wadding, one hundred percent lambs wool, is also used under the skin in detachable collars, cuffs, or fashion detail. The interfilling causes the hair to stand on end and gives the fur a full, rounded appearance.

Leather softener. Combined with water and used for nailing. The solution revives used pelts. It is not used on new skins. The proportions should be ½ cup of leather softener to 3½ cups of water.

Lining. The lining of a used garment may be serviceable if it is cleaned and shows no sign of wear. When selecting new fabric for lining, choose one which is soft. Silk, acetate chromespun, acetate satin, faille, brocade, and twill may be used in a color and pattern which enhances the fur.

Muslin. Used to make a cloth pattern of the garment. All fitting is done on the muslin and corrections are transferred to the paper pattern.

Paper. Brown or newsprint paper used for cutting a pattern for fur collars, cuffs, and fashion details.

Patterns. Furrier's patterns can be obtained from a fur supply house. Dressmaker jacket, coat, and stole patterns may be used if they have simple lines. The ⅝ in. seam allowance is removed from the pattern pieces.

Pellon. A crushproof synthetic felt which gives shape and/or stiffness to collars and cuffs. Size No. 50 is recommended.

Sealing wax. Melted black sealing wax is used to emphasize the nose of a mink pelt in a neck scarf (Figure 24). The wax is obtainable at a stationery store.

Seam binding. Used where less bulk is desired to stay the outer edges, pockets, darts, buttonholes, and occasionally to encase edges. Where the tape shows, the color should harmonize with both the fur and the lining.

Shoulder pads. Used to improve the fit of the garment and to follow the style of the garment.

Stay cloth. A thin, strong, lightweight fabric sewed directly to the skin side for reinforcement. China silk and sheath lining are excellent.

Stud pin. A metal fastener consisting of a long shank end and a spring catch-end, used to make fur detachable (Figure 25). The shank end is sewn on or under the lining and goes through the fabric on which the fur is worn.

Thread. Wax-treated thread does not twist or snarl. Heavy-duty cotton thread or cotton left twist 4 cord may also be used.

Tipping dye. A dye applied with a small paintbrush to the skin of a pelt so that its light color does not show through the fur.

Twill tape. A ⅝ in. cotton tape used in a manner similar to seam binding.

Underlining. Cotton flannel underlining sewn directly to the lining. The two fabrics are treated as one. A low grade outing flannel may be used. It must be soft and have little body.

Velvet ribbon. A rayon velvet ribbon is used on the underside of a fur boa. The width may vary depending upon the size of the pelt. The 2 in. width is most widely used.

Water. Used alone when nailing new mink skins into desired shapes. Used with leather softener and applied with a sponge on used furs when they are nailed out.

4

GENERAL
TECHNIQUES

The general techniques for sewing fur are marking, cutting, nailing, and sewing. The quality of the finished garment depends on the mastery of these techniques.

CUTTING

When cutting fur, be careful to cut only the skin. Avoid cutting the hair. When a cut is properly made, the skin edge should be smooth with the hair extending beyond the cut edge (Figure 26, A and B).

Equipment.
A sharp single-edge razor blade or a furrier's knife.

Procedure.
Cut from the skin side of the pelt.

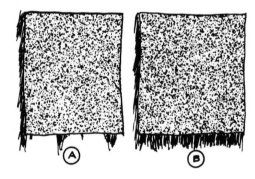

Figure 26

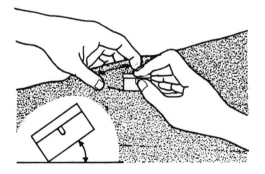

Figure 27

Hold the skin side in one hand, grasping the pelt firmly between the thumb and the fourth finger on the bottom and between the second and third fingers on the top (Figure 27).

Hold the razor blade in the other hand like a pencil.

Draw the tip of the blade through the skin which is held between the two sets of fingers. The heel of the hand rests on the table with the fur off the table (Figure 27).

Most cuts are made toward oneself with as long a sweep as possible.

The blade may be reversed (pointing away from yourself) for short cuts.

After the cut has been made, gently pull the two sections of the skin apart. Tears may occur if the skin is cut or pulled apart too quickly.

NAILING

The purpose of nailing is to take out or obtain shape in a fur. In this process, moisture is applied to the skin side and the fur is temporarily attached to a wooden surface.

Nailing is done on new furs, used furs, and in replacement areas. A discussion of nailing new fur is found in Chapter 6. When used fur is nailed before cutting the new garment pieces, it is done to "press" out the wrinkles and irregularities. When worn areas are replaced with new fur areas, nailing is done to make the pelt smooth and flat. The replacement becomes inconspicuous from the hair side.

Equipment.
Nailing board.

No. 18 brads, staples, or push pins.

Hammer.

Pliers.

Wetting solution: water and/or leather softener.

Cardboard.
1. Strips—½ in. x 12 in. to 18 in.
2. Pieces—approximately 8 in. x 12 in.

Sponge.

Procedure.
Prepare the wetting solution.

1. Mix ½ cup of leather softener in 3½ cups of warm water. (A quart jar is a convenient container in which to mix the solution. Any remaining solution may be stored in the covered jar for future time.) Or,
2. Put warm water in a bowl.

Place the used fur on the nailing board with the skin side up.

Sponge the wetting solution on the entire skin side of the fur.

1. The amount of wetting solution used will depend on the dryness and thickness of the skin.
2. The skin should be wet enough to give it stretch and pliability, but not saturated. The fur side should be dry.

Pin-baste the used fur to the nailing board with the push pins about 3 in. apart. Fill in the spaces with additional pins about 1 in. apart.

Maneuver the skin with the flat side of the hand to extend extra fullness to the outer edges. Work from the center of each piece of fur and do not pull the edges.

Fasten the edges to the nailing board with brads or staples placed 1 in. apart. Keep the edges even.

1. When using a stapler, point the stapler to the outside edge, working out all excess fullness.
2. When using brads, hold the brad in one hand between the middle finger and thumb. Hammer the brad in the board at a slightly outward angle so that the fur will not strain against the brad as it dries (Figure 28).

Replace the push pins with brads or staples (Figure 29).

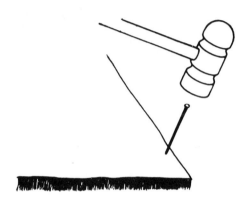

Figure 28

NOTE: If the skin is very tender and seems to separate, place ½ in. wide strips of cardboard over the edges. Put push pins through the cardboard and the skin.

Pieces of cardboard should also be placed over extremely uneven sections of the skin. Push pins, brads, or staples are used to hold both the cardboard and fur to the nailing board (Figure 29). Weight, such as an iron or several books, may be placed on top of the cardboard to help flatten the skin.

Allow the fur pieces to dry slowly. Direct heat should not be used on the skin.

NOTE: The amount of time needed for drying will depend on the thickness of the skin, the amount of wetting solution, and the humidity of the room. On the average, allow approximately twelve hours for drying a complete fur garment of muskrat, mouton lamb, rabbit, or Persian lamb.

Remove the brads or staples with a pliers or stapler remover. Work carefully to avoid tearing the skin.

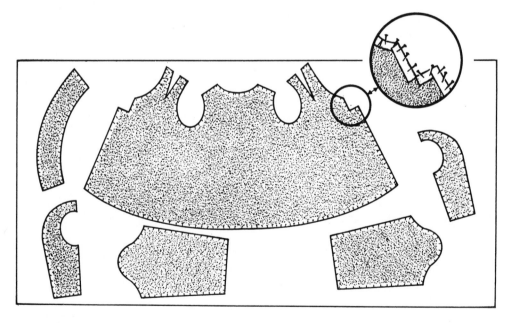

Figure 29

To avoid wrinkles, fold the fur in as few lengthwise folds as possible.

MARKING

Equipment.
Glass-head pins.

Ball-point pen or wax (tailor's) chalk.

Straightedge.

Procedure.
Mark the center back.

1. Method One: striped fur (Figure 30).
   a) Push the glass-head pins through the center stripe on the hair side.
   b) Turn the fur to the skin side.
   c) With ball-point pen or wax chalk, draw a straight line connecting the pin points.
2. Method Two: solid color fur, including curly and straight hair fur.
   a) Fold the used garment shell, hair side out, along the center of the back.
   b) Push the glass-head pins through the fold.
   c) Proceed as in last two steps in section above.

Mark for replacement.

1. Indicate the worn area of the hair side by pushing glass-head pins through the pelt (Figure 31, A).
2. Use chalk or a pen to draw straight or curved lines to connect the pin points (Figure 31, B).

Mark the area used for replacement.

1. Indicate the location of the strips, if any, by pushing glass-head pins through the pelt.
2. Match the stripe location of the

Figure 30

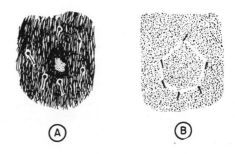

Ⓐ   Ⓑ

Figure 31

worn area with that of the replacement area.
3. Mark the shape of the new replacement area by pushing glass-head pins through the pelt to make an accurate pattern.
4. Draw straight or curved lines to connect the pin points. (See Chapter 5 on Replacing, pp. 97–98.)

Mark the pattern for cutting.

1. Turn the fur to the skin side.
2. Use chalk or a pen to mark around the outside edge of the pattern pieces.

Mark the cut edges for joining.

1. Butt the two cut edges in the exact location.

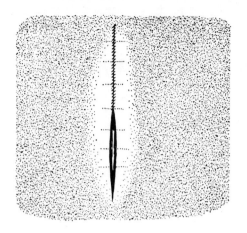

Figure 32

2. Make horizontal marks across the edges every 3 to 4 in.

   NOTE: Horizontal marks serve the same purpose as notches in dressmaker patterns. The marks must match when the seam is sewn together (Figure 32).

SEWING

Most sewing on fur is done from the skin side. The two pieces of fur are held together securely in one hand between the thumb and first two fingers. In sewing, proceed from right to left with even stitches.

Sewing is done on the hair side when closing the tail end of a mink skin for a neck scarf. This includes sewing the rear legs together, the tail, and the bottom edge of the pelt. Velvet ribbon is sewn on the underside of the pelts when making boas.

Equipment.
Needles.

Thimble.

Supplies.
Fur.

Seam tape.

Twill tape.

Cold tape.

Stay cloth.

Lining.

Underlining.

Interfacing.

Interfilling.

Grosgrain ribbon.

Stitches.
Buttonhole stitch (Figure 33).

1. The buttonhole stitch is used to attach snaps to fur collars and to attach crocheted hooks and eyes to the ends of boas.
2. Insert the needle into the fur or fabric and through the opening in either the ball or socket side of a snap.
3. The needle goes through a loop of thread with a single twist.
4. Pull the thread to form a purl at the outside edge of the snap and/or hook and eye.
5. Make four stitches in each of the openings found on either side of the snap or hook and eye.

Catch stitch (Figure 34).

1. The catch stitch is used to attach seam or twill tape to the outer edge of fur garment pieces, to sew darts in the lining, and to sew tape to pockets and buttonhole openings.
2. Work from left to right with the needle pointed toward the left. Be sure the thread is inconspicuous from the hair side of the fur.

Diagonal basting (Figure 35).

1. Diagonal basting is used to attach stay cloth to the skin side of the pelt, to hold the front of the gar-

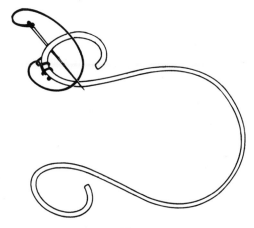

Figure 33

Figure 34

Figure 35

ment to the facing, and to hold the upper and under collars together.

2. Work in horizontal rows from right to left. Hide the short vertical stitch in the hair with the diagonal stitch on top of the stay cloth. A short vertical stitch holds two sections of the garment together and the longer diagonal stitch is found between the skin side of the front facing and interfacing.

Running catch stitch (Figure 36).

1. The running catch stitch is used to sew seam or twill tape to the out-

side edges of the garment pieces or to pocket and buttonhole openings. It is also used to sew the tape in horizontal rows at 6 or 8 in. intervals on the sleeves and the garment shell for reinforcement.

2. Work from right to left with the needle pointed toward the left. Keep the bite small and inconspicuous from the fur side.

Slant hemming (Figure 37).

1. Slant hemming is used to sew seam or twill tape to the skin side after it has been attached to the skin with a whipping stitch. It is also used to sew velvet ribbon to the hair side of a boa on the upper curve.

2. Take equidistant slanting stitches, catching a small amount of the skin and a few threads of the tape in each stitch. The needle should point toward the thumb of one hand as it comes through.

Figure 36

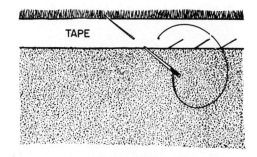

TAPE

Figure 37

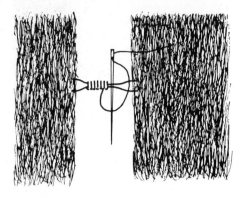

Figure 38

Swing tack (Figure 38).

1. The swing tack is used to hold two mink skins together in a parallel position in a boa neck scarf and to attach two mink skins with the head of one on the back of the other.
2. Using a double thread, take two or three stitches in the two skins, leaving the thread approximately ¾ to 1 in. long. Buttonhole stitch around all the threads, keeping the stitches close together.

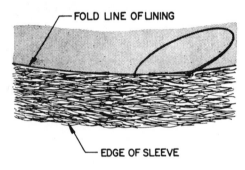

FOLD LINE OF LINING

EDGE OF SLEEVE

Figure 39

Uneven backstitch (Figure 39).

1. The uneven backstitch is used to attach the folded edge of the lining to front fur facings and hem edges, and to adjacent lining sections.
2. Take a stitch from right to left. Point the needle toward the left and bring it up five times the length of the finished stitch. The thread holds the folded edge to the underlying fabric or fur.

Uneven basting stitch (Figure 40).

1. The uneven basting stitch is used to attach the interfacing to a garment front, collar, and cuffs; to hold the interfilling to the skin side of detachable collars, cuffs, or fashion details; to hold interfilling in mink scarves and boas; to sew the seam allowance of the lining to the shell of the coat.

    NOTE: For the above applications, this stitch becomes a permanent stitch and it is not removed from the garment. It is also used on the fur side temporarily, to hold the front facing to the front of a jacket and the under collar to the upper collar.
2. Take a long stitch on top and a short bite into the fur or skin. Work

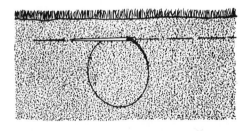

Figure 40

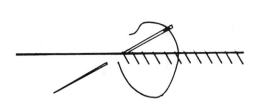

Figure 41

Figure 42

from right to left with the needle pointed toward the left.

Whipping stitch (Figure 41).

1. The whipping stitch is used to hold two pieces of fur together in a seam where there is no reinforcement or where reinforcement such as tape or stay cloth has been used. The whipping stitch is also used to apply seam tape, twill tape, or grosgrain ribbon to the outer edges of pocket openings, buttonholes, and the outer edges of the garment.

2. Use a diagonal stitch. Make the stitch no deeper than necessary to hold the two skin edges together securely (Figure 42). See that the stitches are even in depth and spacing. The tension of the stitch should allow the seam edge to flatten when pressure is applied to the skin side of the fur. As stitches are made, use the needle to push the hair down for a clean seam (Figure 43). Putting a little water on the hair will help to keep it out of the way while sewing. Flatten the seam by rubbing it firmly with a scissors handle (Figure 44). The two skin edges will then butt to form a flat seam.

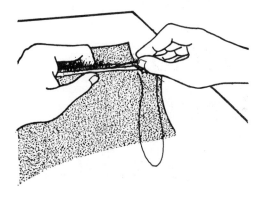

Figure 43

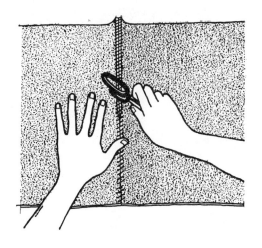

Figure 44

5

RESTYLING JACKETS, COATS, AND STOLES

DISASSEMBLING THE ORIGINAL GARMENT

Procedure.

The first step in restyling a fur garment is to open the original garment.

Remove the lining.

1. Unfasten the lining at the hemline and sleeves, sides, and neckline.
2. Remove the stitches from the underarm, shoulder, and armscye seams.

Open the fur shell.

1. Remove the stitches holding the front facing to the coat.
2. Remove the stitches which hold the under and upper collar together.
3. Open all construction seams: the shoulder, neckline, armscye, underarm, cuff, bustline dart, and fashion detail darts sometimes found in sleeves.
4. Remove the pocket and the facing.
5. Remove all of the stay cloth (usually black cotton fabric) which has been sewn to the skin side (Figure 45).
6. If the edges have been taped, remove all of the tape.

    NOTE: The fine sawdust material often found in the folds of a fur garment is ground tropical nutshells on which the cleaning solvent was placed and not completely removed when the garment was cleaned. Remove this residue carefully; it will make a hard-surfaced floor slippery if dropped.

PREPARATION FOR NAILING

After the original garment is completely disassembled, sew the pocket openings together. This is the only cutting and sewing done before the gar-

Figure 45

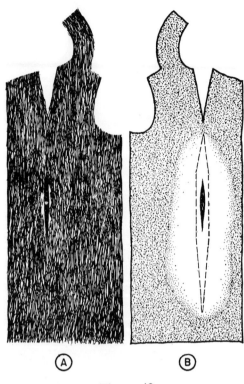

Ⓐ　　　　　Ⓑ

Figure 46

ment shell is nailed. Because it is not always known where worn areas may occur in the new garment, replace worn fur after the new garment pieces are cut.

Equipment and Supplies.

Needle.

Soap crayon, or ball-point pen.

Thread.

Cutting tool.

Straightedge.

Glass-head pins.

Procedure.
Check pocket openings for worn areas. If the opening shows no adjacent worn area, sew it together with the whipping stitch.

If a pocket area shows wear, mark the area with pins from the hair side (Figure 46, A).

Turn the fur to the skin side.

Note the placement of the pins indicating the worn areas.

Mark the worn areas adjacent to the pocket opening with parallel lines (Figure 46, B).

Draw diagonal lines from the ends of the parallel lines to points 12, 18, or 24 in. above and below them. The length of the diagonal lines depends on the width between the parallel lines. The wider the space, the longer the diagonal lines. A double pointed dart has been developed.

Cut out the marked area.

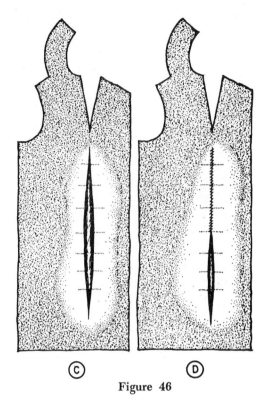

Ⓒ   Ⓓ

Figure 46

Mark the cut edges with perpendicular lines every 4 in. (Figure 46, C).

Start in the middle of the opening and sew it closed (Figure 46, D). Match all the perpendicular markings. There should be no large pucker at either end of the dart. If a large pucker does occur, open the seam and hold the skin edges more evenly. A small pucker will shrink out during nailing.

Press the seam flat with the handle of a shears.

NAILING THE ORIGINAL GARMENT SECTIONS

Equipment and Supplies (see p. 83).

Procedure (see p. 83).

Sequence for nailing.

Garment shell (Figure 47, A).

1. Neck edge of center back.
2. Bottom center back, 3 to 4 in. on each side.
3. Lower right corner, front and bottom edges.
4. Lower left corner, front and bottom edges.
5. Top right shoulder edge.
6. Top left shoulder edge.
7. Front edges.
8. Armscyes.

Sleeves (Figure 47, B).

1. Cap of sleeve.
2. Bottom of sleeve.
3. Underarm seam working from top to bottom.

Collar (Figure 47, C).

1. Neck edge of center back.
2. Outside edge of center back.
3. Side edges.

CUTTING OUT THE NEW GARMENT

It is important to remember that the fur for the new garment be the best available and require as little replacing as possible.

To determine the location of the pattern pieces for the new garment, check the hair side of the fur for areas having the least amount of worn fur. If there are no worn areas, the pattern pieces should be laid on the corresponding pieces of the used garment. If worn areas do occur in the new garment, the pattern pieces may be shuffled so that replacement will be kept at a minimum. In most instances, the new garment will be smaller than the original. When two used garments of similar fur are pieced together, the new garment may be larger.

Procedure.
Determine the center back of the used fur shell from the hair side. Push glass-

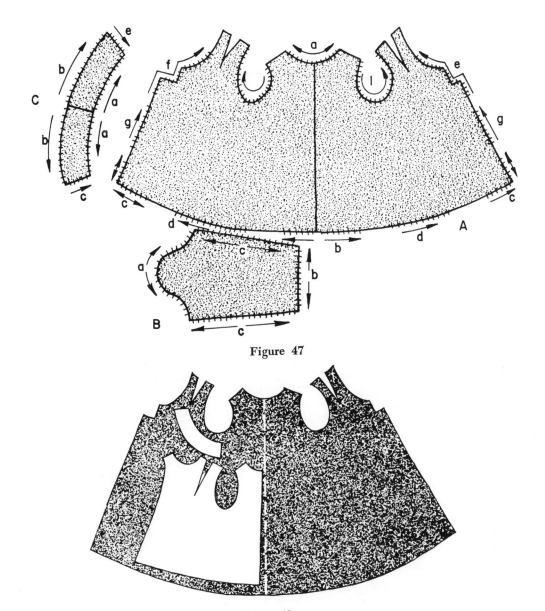

Figure 47

Figure 48

head pins through the center stripe. When there are no stripes, fold shell in center back and push pins through fold.

Turn the fur to the skin side.

Draw a straight line connecting the pin marks.

Lay all the pattern pieces on the used fur.

NOTE: Place the pattern on the skin side in order to use the lower sweep of the old garment for the bottom edge of the new garment. When using any fur which has a horizontal pelt line, the bottom row of pelts should be wide enough to eliminate a chopped-off appearance.

1. Place the pattern front and back on the used fur shell (Figure 48).
   a) Place the center back of the

Figure 49

pattern on the center back marking.

b) Mark one half of the pattern on the skin side.

c) Reverse the pattern and mark the remaining side.

d) Check the location of the stripes. They must run parallel to the center front and the center back.

e) Check the direction of the fur. It must run parallel to the center front and the center back.

f) Slash the pattern at the underarm seam line if the front edge of the pattern runs diagonally to the stripe or direction of the hair (Figure 49).

g) If a striped fur is used, a dark stripe is preferable for the center front edge.

h) When using fur with horizontal pelt lines such as the zigzag line found in muskrat, rabbit, and marmot, the lines must be matched at corresponding seam lines.

i) Mark the location of the front fold line with a contrasting colored uneven basting thread.

2. Place the sleeve pattern piece on the used fur sleeve. Be sure to re-

Figure 50

verse the sleeve pattern in order to make a pair of sleeves (Figure 50).

3. Place the collar pattern pieces on pieces of good used fur. See the special instructions below for cutting fur.

4. Place the cuff pattern pieces on good used fur or on the used fur cuffs.

Pin the pattern pieces to the skin side of the fur.

Mark around the outer edge of all of the

pattern pieces with soap crayon or a ball-point pen.

Cut out the pattern pieces.

Cutting a Collar from Striped or Straight Haired Fur

A collar must be darted when using straight haired fur or fur with a simulated grotzen line (a line painted on the fur and often found naturally on muskrat, squirrel, and rabbit). Darting the fur permits the stripe or direction of hair to follow the collar curve. The stripe must match in the center back.

Procedure.
Slash the collar pattern at the neck edge curve (Figure 51, A and B).

Place the outer edge of the pattern on the straight direction or stripe of the fur (Figure 51, C). This method will form open darts at the neck edge of the collar.

Mark the fur.

Cut the fur.

Optional Method.

1. Pattern pieces may be placed on the fur so that the straight hair or stripe seems to be radiating from the center. The stripes must match on either side of the collar (Figure 52).
2. If curly fur is used, the collar pattern need not be darted (Figure 53).

Optional Method for Cutting Out a Fur Garment

Because of the location of the worn areas, it may be necessary to adjust the

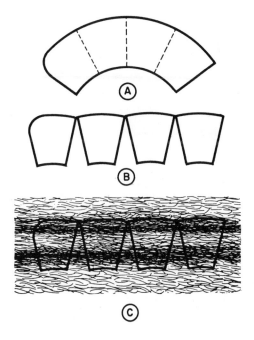

Figure 51

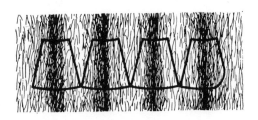

Figure 52

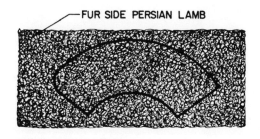

Figure 53

Figure 54

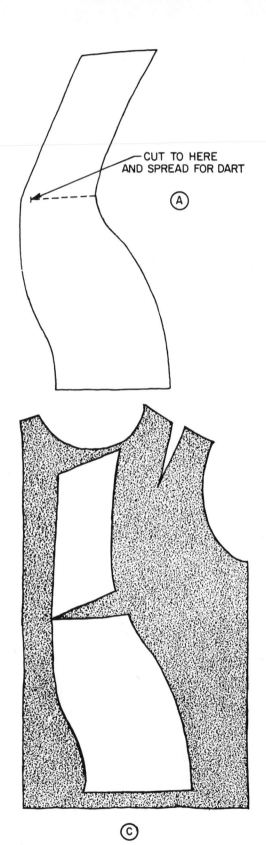

CUT TO HERE
AND SPREAD FOR DART

(A)

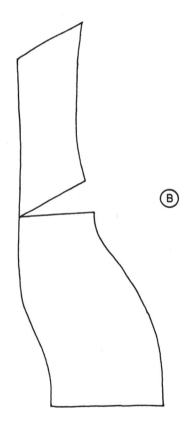

(B)

(C)

Figure 55

placement of the pattern pieces (Figure 54). The front edges of the pattern may be placed on the underarm seam of the used garment. The underarm area of a used garment usually shows the least amount of wear and oxidation. The center back of the pattern may be placed on the center front with a center back seam. The fronts of the new garment are then placed on the least worn used fur. When new garments are cut in this manner, there will be more construction seams. When the fur is striped, the stripes must match on corresponding pattern pieces.

A garment may have very full sleeves of good used fur. They may be used for the pattern front and back.

Cutting Out a Stole

It is difficult to say whether the direction of the hair should flow up or down on a stole. The style of the stole and the amount of used fur will help to determine the decision. Many interesting effects may be obtained by using the fur so that the direction of the hair flows at different angles (but it should flow at the same angle on corresponding pattern pieces). In the present trend, hair runs up on mink stoles and the hair of similar furs may also run up. Curly furs, such as Persian lamb, broadtail, and karakul, have a less noticeable hair direction. If the fur has a stripe, it is important to have all stripes match.

The following procedure is used with fur having straight hair. When using a one-piece stole pattern as shown in Figure 55, A, you must split the pattern as shown in Figure 55, B. Place the altered pattern on the skin side (Figure 55, C). In this way the direction of the guard, or outer, hair will run parallel to the center front and across the center back.

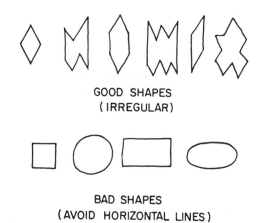

GOOD SHAPES
(IRREGULAR)

BAD SHAPES
(AVOID HORIZONTAL LINES)

Figure 56

REPLACING OR PATCHING

Replacing must be inconspicuous. It can be more noticeable in straight hair fur than curly hair fur. Vertical seams are the least conspicuous in straight haired fur. Straight horizontal seams should be avoided whenever possible. Zigzag seams must be used in replacing if they have been used in the original garment. Careful matching of fur with respect to color, direction, and density will help to make replacements less noticeable. Desirable and undesirable shapes for replacing are shown in Figure 56.

The amount of replacing will depend on the amount of fur left after the garment is cut out. Replacing worn fur areas is done after the new garment is cut out. See "Marking," p. 85.

Procedure.
Check the garment pieces for replacement areas.

Determine the shape of the replacement areas.

1. Make the replacement area irregular in shape. Diamond shaped re-

placements are used in worn button areas.

2. When a large section has several worn areas, replace the whole section, rather than making several small replacements.

3. Make the replacement the length of the pelt if possible.

Mark the replacement areas.

Cut out the marked areas.

Use the cut-out piece of fur as a pattern for the replacement piece.

Mark the replacement piece.

Cut out the replacement piece.

Sew the replacement piece into position.

Flatten the seam.

Nail out the replacement area if necessary.

1. Place the fur skin side up on the nailing board, keeping the replacement piece and surrounding area flat.

2. Dampen the replacement piece and the surrounding area with warm water and a sponge.

3. Place a piece of cardboard over the dampened area.

4. Use push pins to fasten the cardboard and the fur to the nailing board (Figure 57).

5. Allow the fur to dry from four to eight hours.

6. Remove the push pins and the cardboard from the fur and nailing board.

DYEING

Some fur dyeing may be done successfully at home, but the results cannot be guaranteed. Color oxidation is usually covered by dye restoring the fur to an even color. The dye should be darker than the original color. Thus, a light brown may be changed to a medium brown and a medium brown to a dark brown. In general, bleached fur does not dye successfully. Dyeing will help to camouflage the appearance of worn areas. Dye is applied after the garment pieces are cut out and all replacing is completed. Use one of the following methods for dyeing fur.

Brush Dyeing.
Brush dyeing is done with a vegetable fiber brush (Figure 58). The fur dye is obtainable at a fur supply company and

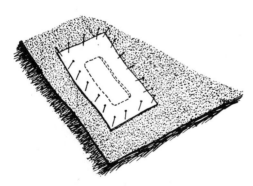

Figure 57

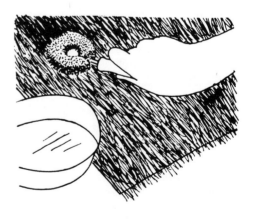

Figure 58

comes in various shades of brown and gray, and in black.

Prepare the dye.

1. Obtain dye as close as possible to the time of application. After dye bottles are opened, the contents begin to lose strength.
2. Pour equal quantities of dye and fixative into a glass bowl. Do not use metal containers.
3. Prepare the dye solution in small quantities.
   a) Place several layers of newspapers on a flat surface.
   b) Place all of the garment pieces on the paper, hair side up.
   c) Wear rubber gloves and a coverall apron.
   d) Use a fiber vegetable brush to apply dye to the hair.
   e) Apply dye with the direction of the hair, starting from the top of the garment section. Be sure to cover all of the edges.
   f) Dye all of the garment pieces.
   g) Allow the garment pieces to remain flat until dry, usually overnight.
   h) Do not save any *unused mixed* fur dye. Oxidation takes place and the dye loses strength. Any *unused dye* and *fixative* remaining in the bottles may be saved for a short period of time. Screw the cap on the bottles securely and store them in a cool, dark place. Small areas, particularly seams and edges may have to be touched up after the garment is sewn together.
   i) Some dye will rub off on your hands when constructing the garment. All dyed fur garments should be cleaned, preferably by a professional fur cleaner, before they are worn. In addi-

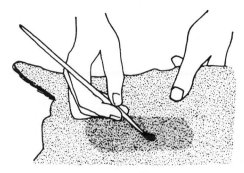

Figure 59

tion to removing the excess dye, cleaning will soften the pelts.

Tipping.

Tipping is a process of dyeing or staining the leather so that it will be nearly the same color as the underfur (Figure 59). It is particularly useful when working with dark fur because of the contrast between the color of the hair and the skin.

Tipping is done on the skin side in the area of the eyes, ears, and legs of mink. It may also be used at the ends of boas or in the area near any cut edge.

Tipping dye is obtainable from fur supply companies. It is applied with a small watercolor paintbrush to the skin side of the fur. Allow the dye to dry thoroughly before sewing.

Touch-up Dyeing.

Touch-up dyeing is done after a garment is sewn together. The method used depends on the size of the area to be touched up.

Large area touch-up dyeing.

Fur dye in aerosol cans is available from fur supply companies. It can be used on garments which do not need a complete dyeing. It may be used on front edges, cuff edges, collar edges, and small oxidized areas. Apply only a small amount of dye at a time so that the dyed area will blend into the adjacent area. Hold the can 12 to 18 in. away from the hair when spraying.

Small area touch-up dyeing.

A permanent ink felt pen may be used to touch up very small areas of off-colored fur. It can also be used if the hair is very thin and the skin is noticeable.

Sometimes a garment is completed before an off-colored area is noticed. A felt pen may be used to color both the skin and the hair. On used black fur, small purple areas may occur. Small areas of gray skin color sometimes occur on black Persian lamb. The use of the black felt pen makes these areas less noticeable.

REINFORCING

Reinforcing adds strength to the skin side of the fur. It is done to the entire skin side, part or parts of the skin side, or the cut edges. It is done on all construction seams, such as underarm seams, sleeve seams, shoulder seams, and darts. Edges are not reinforced on replacements or replacement areas.

Taping.

Taping refers to the attachment of twill seam or cold tape to the skin. It is placed on the outer edges of all garment pieces

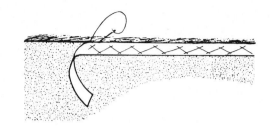

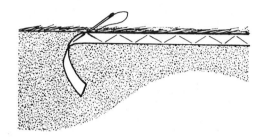

Figure 61

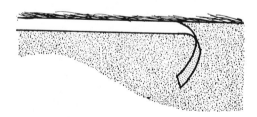

Figure 60

before joining the seams. To give added strength to the skin, rows of twill or seam tape may be sewn across the garment shell and sleeves at 6 to 8 in. intervals.

Cold tape (Figure 60).

1. Apply tape to all cut edges by pressing the adhesive side firmly to the edges on the skin side of the fur.
2. Allow the tape to overlap at the dart points.
3. Slash the tape when applying it to curves so that it follows the shape of the curve. When using cold tape, it is advisable to have the new garment cleaned with the lining attached. The cleaning solvent on the ground tropical nutshells used in cleaning fur causes the tape to loosen.

Twill tape (Figure 61).

1. Use ⅝ in. twill tape.

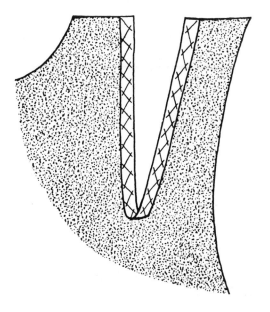

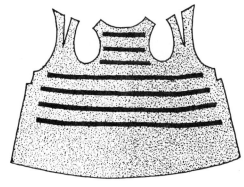

Figure 63

Figure 62

2. Apply tape to all cut edges on the skin side using the catch stitch or running catch stitch (see p. 86–87).
3. Keep the direction of the stitch parallel to the direction of the guard hairs. This will help hide the thread.
    NOTE: The needle should be inserted as in Figure 34, p. 87.
4. Slash the tape if necessary when going around curves to keep it flat.
5. Fold the tape at appropriate angles on corners.
6. Bend the tape around the base of darts so that it forms a pocket (Figure 62).
7. Optional use of tape.
    Twill tape may be used to stay the shell and sleeves of the new garment in a manner similar to stay cloth (Figure 63).
    a) Place the tape in horizontal rows starting near the neck edge.
    b) Space the rows about 6 to 8 in. apart.
    c) Pin the tape to the skin keeping it slightly taut.
    d) Use a running catch stitch or catch stitch to attach the tape.

Seam tape.

1. Seam tape is used in the same way as twill tape.
2. It is used where less bulk is desired on thin-skinned furs such as ermine, squirrel, and mink.
3. It is also used for small accessory pieces.

Staying.
Staying is the application of fabric or a chemical to the entire skin side of the fur for purposes of reinforcement.

Fabric staying.

1. Place a fabric such as china silk or sheath lining over the entire skin

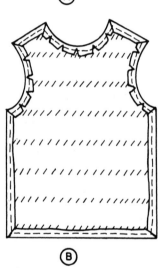

Figure 64

the length of the stitch small on the hair side. The direction of the stitch should be parallel to the direction of the hair to hide the thread in the fur.

Chemical staying.

1. Use a small paintbrush to apply a thin layer of the chemical to the entire skin area.
2. The solution forms a plastic bond with the skin that is permanent and pliable. It is not destroyed in dry cleaning.

ASSEMBLING THE NEW GARMENT

Procedure.
Close the reinforced edges.

1. Before beginning to sew the seams, put the two reinforced edges together in position.
2. Make several crayon or pen marks perpendicular to the cut edges to serve as guides. These marks substitute for the notches found in dressmaker patterns (see Figure 32).
3. When a seam is completed, press it flat by rubbing the handle of a pair of shears over the seam which has been placed on a hard surface (see Figure 44).

   a) Sew the darts.
   b) Sew the front facings to the garment fronts.
   c) Sew the side seams.
   d) Sew the shoulder seams.
   e) Sew the sleeve seams.
   f) Sew the armscye seams.
   g) Sew the center back seam of the upper and under collars.
   h) Sew the under collar to the neck edge of the garment.
   i) Sew the upper collar to the under collar on the outside edge.

side. Do not cut the fabric (Figure 64, A).

2. Attach the fabric with a diagonal basting stitch. Make rows of stitches 2 to 3 in. apart.
3. After the fabric is attached, cut off the excess, allowing a folded edge around the outside edges of the skin (Figure 64, B).
4. Sew the folded edges to the skin with an uneven basting stitch. Keep

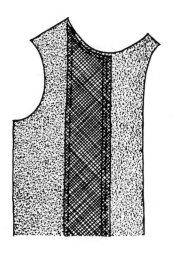

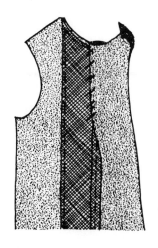

Figure 65   Figure 66   Figure 67

j)   Sew the back neck facing to the bottom edge of the top collar.

k)   Sew the bottom edge of the cuff to the bottom edge of the sleeve.

l)   Sew the cuff seams together.

Attach the interfacings.

1. Front.

   a)   Use furrier's felt, heavy pellon, or a heavy grade of cotton flannel or muslin.

   b)   Cut the interfacing 2 in. wider than the garment facing. OPTIONAL: If the front facing is only 1 to 2 in. wide, the interfacing may be as wide as 6 to 8 in. Do not cover bustline darts with interfacing.

   c)   Make a 1 in. fold the length of the interfacing on the front edge.

   d)   Place the folded edge of the interfacing even with the center front fold line on the skin side.

   e)   Baste, permanently, the folded edge of the interfacing to the garment front with an uneven basting stitch. Keep the stitches *loose*.

   f)   Place a second row of stitches ½ in. from the outside edge of the interfacing. Keep the stitches *loose* (Figure 65).

   g)   Fold the front facing back into position and mark the location for the hooks and eyes. Insert the hooks and eyes (see pp. 106–108).

   h)   Fasten the outer edge of the front facing to the garment after attaching the collar and hooks and eyes.

   i)   Turn the garment to the fur side.
   Fold the front on the center front fold line.
   Baste ½ in. from the front edge, using a contrasting color thread.

   j)   Turn the garment to the skin side. Open the facing and the interfaced front.

   k)   Baste, loosely, 1 in. from the fold using the diagonal basting stitch to attach the facing to the garment front starting at the neckline (Figure 66).

   l)   Repeat the diagonal basting ½ in. from the outside edge of the front facing (Figure 67).

   m)   Remove the basting from the fur side of the front edge.

2. Collar.
   a) Cut the interfacing 1 in. larger than the under collar pattern.
   b) Turn the collar skin side out.
   c) Fold the interfacing 1 in. from the outer edge. Do not fold the inner edge.
   d) Remove any excess fullness of the fold back by slashing.
   e) Baste the folded edge of the interfacing to the under collar, using permanent uneven basting stitches.
   f) If the collar is large, you will need more than one row of basting stitches. The last row should be ½ in. from the neck edge of the collar.
   g) Turn the collar to the hair side and baste ½ in. from the folded edge.
   h) Open the collar to the skin side.
   i) Use a loose diagonal stitch to baste the top collar to the interfaced bottom collar 1 in. from the outer edge.
   j) Baste diagonally near the open neck edge.
      NOTE: Several rows of diagonal basting are necessary if the collar is wide. For a narrow collar, only two rows of basting are required.
   k) Check the collar. The top collar must lie smoothly over the under collar, rolling gently toward the outer edge.
   l) Remove the uneven bastings from the hair side.

3. Cuffs.
   a) Cut the interfacing for the cuffs ½ in. smaller than the fur cuff.
   b) Fasten the interfacing to the skin side of the cuffs with two rows of uneven basting stitches ½ in. from the bottom and top edges of the cuff.

POCKETS

Pockets can be made with a vertical, horizontal, diagonal, or curved opening. The style of the garment will determine which shape opening to use. Most pockets are made with a vertical opening. For a vertical opening, the location is approximately two-thirds the width of the garment front from the front edge (Figure 68). The location of the horizontal, diagonal, and curved pocket opening is determined by the style and proportion of the fur garment.

Procedure.
Prepare the pocket opening.

1. Mark the pocket openings with pins from the hair side of the garment (Figure 68).
2. Turn the fur to the skin side.
3. Mark the length of the opening by connecting the pin points with a straight line.

Stay the pocket openings.

1. Sew 1½ in. strips of twill or seam tape across each end of the pocket opening.
2. Sew tape to the skin on both sides of the pocket opening. Let the ends of the tape extend beyond the tape sewed in Step 1.
3. Cut the pocket opening between the tape.
4. Use either the running catch stitch or catch stitch (Figure 69).
5. Optional method: Cold tape may be used in place of twill or seam tape.

Prepare the pouch. The pouch may be made from lining material, velveteen, or cotton pocketing.

1. Cut a piece of fabric 7 in. by 12 in.
2. Cut two strips of 1 in. grosgrain ribbon 9 in. long.

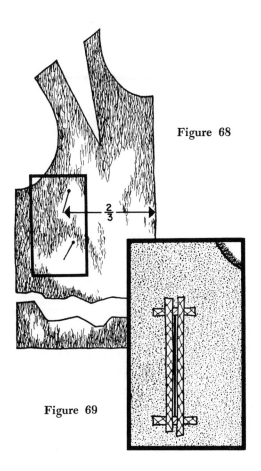

Figure 68

Figure 69

3. On the right side of the fabric, lap the ribbon ¼ in. over the two narrow edges. Ribbon should extend 1 in. beyond either end of the edge (Figure 70).
4. Machine stitch the ribbon to the fabric on the edge of the ribbon.
5. Fold the fabric crosswise with the right sides together (Figure 71).
6. Machine stitch the pouch together in the shape shown in Figure 71.
7. The pouch opening should be the same size as the pocket opening.
8. Trim off excess pouch fabric allowing ½ in. seams. Do not cut off the ribbon.

Sewing the pouch to the pocket opening.

1. Pin the insides of the pouch to the hair sides of the pocket opening.
2. Sew the ribbon of the pouch to the reinforced edge of the fur from the

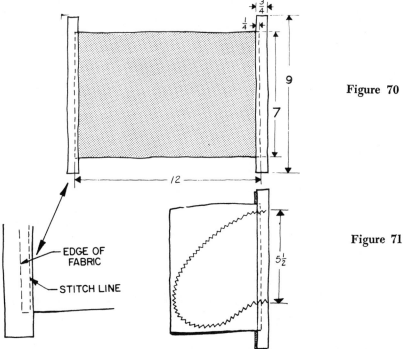

Figure 70

EDGE OF FABRIC

STITCH LINE

Figure 71

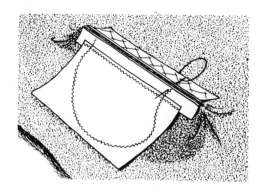

Figure 72

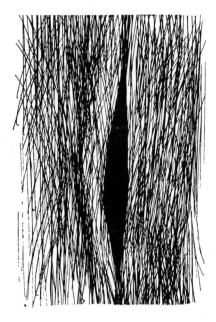

Figure 73

skin side using the whipping stitch beginning at the pocket opening (Figure 72).

3. Turn the pouch toward the center front of the garment.

  a) Keep the two thicknesses of the ribbon together.

  b) Sew the ribbon to the skin.

4. Tack the outer edge of the pouch seam to the skin of the front.

5. When the front facing covers the pouch, tack the facing to one thick-

ness of the pouch or to the seam allowance of the pouch. The width of the front facing will determine where to tack the pouch.

Optional Method.

Fur facing may be used in place of grosgrain ribbon. It may be used for one or both sides of the opening depending upon the bulkiness of the fur. The finished pocket will appear as shown in Figure 73.

CLOSURES

Fashion dictates the type of closure to be used on a fur garment. Generally speaking, a hook-and-eye fastener is placed at the front neck edge and at the waistline of a jacket or coat; however, buttons may be used if you wish. Many stoles do not require a fastener. Covered snaps are used on small fur accessories. Try on the garment to determine location of closures.

Hooks and Eyes.
The hook is placed on the right front of the garment and the eye on the left front. A crocheted ring may be substituted for the eye. Choose closures in the least conspicuous color.

Mark the opening.

1. Mark the location of the hooks and eyes from the fur side with pins.
2. Turn the garment to the skin side.
3. Make a cross with a ball-point pen to mark the hook opening (Figure 74). The vertical line will be parallel to the front edge of the garment. The horizontal line will be parallel to the bottom edge of the garment.
4. Move the mark for the placement of the eye the depth of the eye toward the side seam (Figure 75).

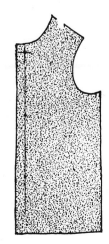

Figure 74

Sew the hook.

1. Insert the hook in the opening from the skin side. The back of the hook will be sewn to the front of the garment.
2. Center the hook on the cross mark.
3. Sew the opening together on either side of the back of the hook and also between the covered wire at the bend of the hook (Figure 76, A).
4. Insert a 3 in. piece of twill tape or seam binding in the hook loops.
5. Pull the hook back so that the bend of the bill hugs the edge of the opening (Figure 76, B).
6. Cross the ends of the tape over each other.
7. Sew the tape to the skin on the right garment front.
8. Check the hook to see that it does not extend over the front edge (Figure 76, C).

Sew the eye.

1. Insert the eye in the opening on the left front of the garment.
2. Center the eye on the cross mark.
3. Sew the opening closed on either

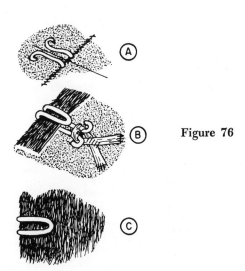

Figure 76

Figure 75

The round end of the eye should be at the center of the cross mark. Make a cross as you did for the hook opening.

Cut the opening. Cut a vertical opening about ½ in. long. The center of the opening will be at the horizontal arm of the cross.

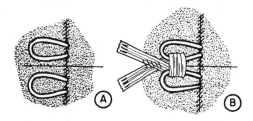

Figure 77

side of the loops and between the loops (Figure 77, A).

4. Insert a 3 in. piece of twill or seam tape in the end loops of the eye.
5. Cross the ends of the tape over each other.
6. Sew the tape to the skin on the left front of the garment (Figure 77, B).
7. Check the eye from the fur side to see that the loop is far enough out of the opening so that the hook will pass through it easily.

Sew the crocheted ring.

1. Insert a 3 in. piece of twill or seam tape through the ring.
2. Pull the ends of the tape through the opening to the skin side.
3. Bring the edge of the ring to the cut edge of the skin.
4. Cross the ends of the tape.
5. Sew the tape to the skin.

Snaps.

If snaps are used, usually a large size (No. 4) is selected. A covered snap is the least conspicuous. Covered snaps can be purchased, or they can be covered with a strong lightweight fabric the same color as the fur. Lining fabric may be used.

1. Sew a small piece of stay cloth on the skin side.
2. Sew the snap on the hair side of the fur with a buttonhole stitch (Figure 33).

Buttonholes.

Mark the location of the buttonhole from the hair side by pushing a pin through the skin at the outer edges of the button.

Turn the garment to the skin side.

Using a ball-point pen or crayon, mark the length of the buttonhole by connecting the pin points with a straight line.

Cut the skin for the opening.

Sew a 2 in. strip of seam or twill tape across each end of the openings, using the catch stitch or running catch stitch.

Cut two pieces of tape the length of the buttonhole plus 2 in. Center the tape and sew flat to each side of the opening.

Turn the garment to the fur side (Figure 78).

Sew a grosgrain ribbon or seam binding, using the whipping stitch, to the cut edges, leaving 1 in. of ribbon or tape free at each end.

Turn the fur to the skin side.

Slash the interfacing the width of the buttonhole.

Pull the second tape through the fur and interfacing.

Hem the tape to the interfacing (Figure 78).

On the facing side, the second tape is hemmed to the skin.

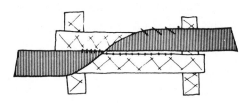

Figure 78

Sew the tapes of the two finished buttonholes together and pull the thread securely, using a diagonal basting stitch (Figure 79).

Buttons.

Fur buttons may be made with metal or plastic button forms, available at the notion counter in department or variety stores.

Thin-skinned fur should be slightly dampened on the skin side and stretched over the form.

To make a fuller looking button, sew two pieces of fur together with the guard hair running toward each other.

The back of the button form is clamped into position. Even if the skin is not pliable and is somewhat thick, a fur button can be made with wooden button forms or the shaped sections of the metal or plastic button form.

Place the button form on the skin side of a piece of fur.

Draw a circle ½ in. larger than the mold.

Sew tape to the edge of the fur circle (Figure 80, A).

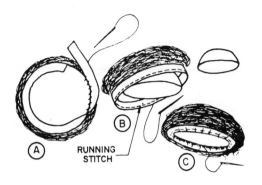

Figure 80

Sew small running stitches along the free edge of the tape.

Place the button mold on the circle, draw up the thread (Figure 80, B), and fasten it securely.

Sew a small piece of felt or fabric to the skin side of the fur to reinforce the area.

Sew on the button (Figure 80, C).

EDGES

When working with edges, tape or ribbon is sewn to the hair side of the fur and piping is sewn to the skin side. Linings are sewn to the ribbon, tape, or piping. Furriers use the term "bend-back" taping, which refers to the attachment of tape or ribbon to all outside edges from the fur side. The tape is turned back to the skin side and sewn. The outside edges include fur collars and cuffs of fabric coats and suits, cuffs of fur garments, and the bottom edges of a fur jacket, coat, or stole.

The type of hair, whether curly or straight, its thickness, and the location of the edge must be taken into consideration when determining which method will be used to conceal the thickness of the skin. More than one method may be used in a single garment. If a rolled or full edge is desired, use the tape

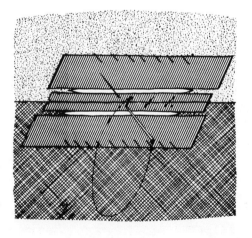

Figure 79

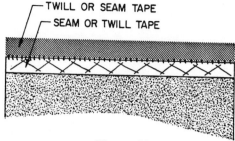

Figure 81

method. If a flat edge is desired, use the grosgrain ribbon or piping method.

Tape.

Tape is used to conceal the outer edge of cuffs, the outer and inner edges of detachable cuffs, collars, and accessories, and the bottom edge of sleeves and garments (Figure 81).

1. Use ⅝ in. twill tape or seam tape. (Seam tape is used on mink, rabbit, fitch, and squirrel.)
2. Reinforce the edge with seam, twill, or cold tape on the skin side.
3. Place the tape on the hair side and sew it to the fur with a whipping stitch. Sew with an even tension: if the tape is sewn too loosely, it will be wavy; if it is sewn too tightly, the fur will cup inward toward the skin side.
4. Bend the reinforced edge of the skin and sew the tape to the skin with an uneven basting stitch or a hemming stitch (Figure 81). In this method the fur is bent around the edge of the first tape. Figures 82 and 84 show a cross section of the tapes and skin.

Grosgrain Ribbon.

Grosgrain ribbon is used on mouton, Persian lamb, and other curly haired fur. It is also used on long straight haired fur in stoles on the center front edges.

1. Use ⅝ in. grosgrain ribbon which matches the color of the fur (Figure 83).

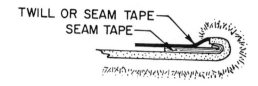

Figure 82

2. Reinforce the edge with seam, twill, or cold tape from the skin side (see p. 100).
3. Sew the grosgrain ribbon to the hair side with the whipping stitch, keeping the tension even.
4. Sew from right to left with the skin side facing you. The needle goes through ribbon, fur, and tape.
5. Turn *only* the grosgrain ribbon over the edge and fasten it to the skin with uneven basting stitches. The edge must be flat (Figure 84).
6. A narrow row of grosgrain ribbon shows from the hair side.

Piping.

Piping is used on the bottom edge of a garment made from long haired fur such as muskrat, mink, and rabbit. When the direction of the hair is downward, it is not necessary to apply tape to the bottom edge.

1. Cut strips of lining fabric 2 in. wide and as long as necessary. The strip

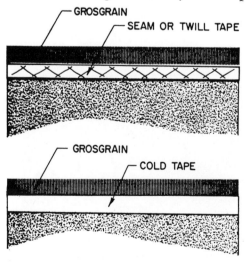

Figure 83

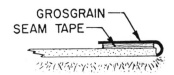

Figure 84

does not need to be cut on the bias.

2. Fold the strip lengthwise in the middle and press it.
3. Place the folded edge of the piping $\frac{1}{16}$ in. beyond the skin edge at the bottom, beginning at the edge of the front facing. Conceal the raw edge of the piping by placing the edges under the facing, or turning under the raw edges.
4. Sew the piping to the skin with a diagonal basting stitch (Figure 85). Put the needle into the piping about $\frac{1}{8}$ in. from the fold and through the skin as close to the cut edge as possible. To conceal the thread on the hair side, the stitch should run parallel with the hair.
5. Sew the lining to the piping. The lining covers the diagonal basting stitches.

LINING AND UNDERLINING

Fabric for lining should be soft. Used fabric may be serviceable, but it must show no signs of wear or oxidation. Before cutting the used lining, it should be washed or dry cleaned.

Use the garment pattern for the back, sleeves, cuffs, and front. Subtract the fac-

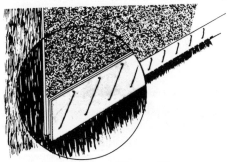

Figure 85

ing from the front pattern. If the collar is double, it requires no lining; but single collars must be lined.

General Directions.
Cutting the lining from a new fabric.

1. Place the pattern pieces on the fabric with the grain running lengthwise. Allow 1 in. around the outer edge of each pattern piece (Figure 86). Place the center back

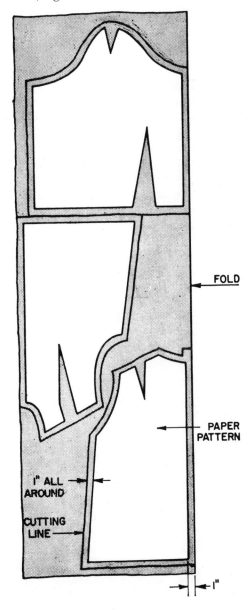

FOLD

PAPER PATTERN

1" ALL AROUND

CUTTING LINE

1"

Figure 86

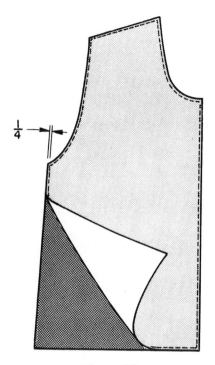

Figure 87

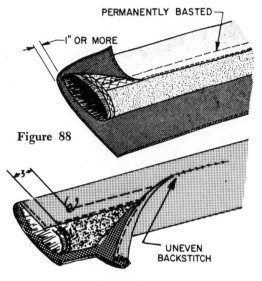

Figure 88

Figure 89

of the pattern 1 in. from the fold.

2. Pin the pattern to the fabric and cut out the lining.

3. *Do not cut out the darts.*

Cutting the lining from the original lining.

1. Rip apart the original lining seams and darts.

2. Place the pattern pieces on the corresponding pieces of the original lining.

3. Proceed in the manner described for new fabric.

Cutting the underlining.

1. Choose an underlining fabric which is soft. If furriers' underlining is not available, use inexpensive cotton flannel.

2. The underlining is cut exactly like the lining.

Procedure.

Prepare the lining.

1. Place the corresponding pieces of lining on the nap side of the underlining.

2. Pin the lining to the underlining along the edges, smoothing it out from the center.

3. Machine stitch ¼ in. from the outer edge around the lining pieces (Figure 87).

Attach the lining to the garment.

1. Line the sleeve.

   a) Turn the garment sleeve skin side out.

   b) Place the wrong side of the lining on the skin side.

   c) Pin the back seam allowance of the sleeve lining over the front side of the seam of the garment.

   d) Baste permanently, keeping the stitches loose. Leave 3 in. free at the bottom of the sleeve (Figure 88).

   e) Turn the front seam allowance of the lining under and pin the folded edge to the lining, covering the basting stitches made in *d*.

   f) Hem the folded edge to the

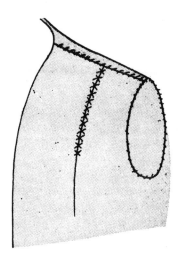

Figure 90

lining with the uneven backstitch (Figure 89).

g) Pin the cap of the sleeve over
the armhole seam.

h) Permanently baste the sleeve
lining over the garment armhole seam, keeping the stitches
loose.

i) Turn the seam allowance under at the bottom edge.

j) Pin.

NOTE: The bottom of the
sleeve lining will be sewn later
after fitting (see note p. 114).

2. Line the back.

a) When pinning the lining to the
fur garment, it is helpful to
place the garment, skin side
out, over a dress form or chair.
If the lining is too tight, it will
cause wrinkles.

b) Pin the back lining to the skin
side of the garment back (Figure 90). The shoulder seam allowance should extend 1 in. beyond the front of the garment.
The back side seam allowance
should extend 1 in. beyond the
front of the garment at the
seam line.

c) Baste permanently the lining
back to the garment at the

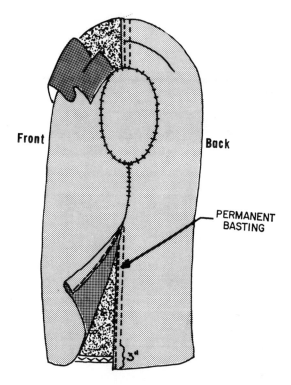

Front **Back**

PERMANENT
BASTING

Figure 91

shoulder and side seams. Keep
the basting *loose*.

d) Turn under the edges at the
back of the armscye. Clip where
necessary.

e) Pin extra fullness in the center back into a pleat.

f) Turn the lining under at the
neck edge and pin it. It may
be necessary to slash the seam
allowance at this edge in front
to have a flat fold. (This edge
is hemmed when the front lining is sewn to the garment.)

3. Line the front.

a) Fold the dart toward the center front and pin it (Figure 91).

b) Place the lining dart over the
garment dart and pin them together.

c) Turn the front shoulder seam
allowance under 1 in. and pin
it at the shoulder line. This fold
is placed on top of the garment

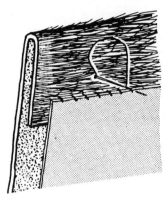

Figure 92

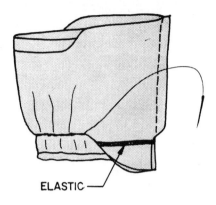

ELASTIC

Figure 93

shoulder seam. It may be necessary to cut out some of the folded lining and underlining under the dart to reduce bulk in the fold.

d) Hem the shoulder seam.

e) Turn the side seam allowance under 1 in. and pin it to the seam allowance of the lining back. The edge of the lining turn is on top of the garment side seam. If there is no side seam, place the folded edge of lining where there would be a side seam.

f) Hem the side seam.

g) Turn the front edge of the lining under.

h) Pin the folded edge to the hair side of the front facing.

i) Fold under the neck edge of the lining and pin it to the garment. It may be necessary to slash the seam allowance to fit the lining smoothly.

j) Hem the lining front and the neck edges to the garment (Figure 92).

4. Hem the lower edge of the lining.
 NOTE: Try on the garment. Pin the lining at the bottom of the garment and the sleeves about 8 in. above the lower edges.

a) Turn under the lower edge of the lining front and back.

b) Pin the lining to the garment.

c) Try the garment on before hemming. If the lining is too tight, wrinkles and cupping of the fur will result. Release the pins and allow ease in the lining.

d) Hem the lining hem to the grosgrain ribbon, piping, or seam tape on the sweep of the garment with the uneven back stitch.

5. Line the cuffs.

a) Baste permanently one side seam allowance of the lining to the skin side of the cuff seam to within $\frac{1}{2}$ in. of the ends of the cuff.

b) Bring the lining around the cuff. Fold under the other side-seam allowance and lap the folded edge over the previous basting.

c) Hem the lining seam the length of the cuff.

d) Turn under the top edge of the cuff lining at the fur edge of the cuff.

e) Pin the lining to the cuff.

f) Attach the lining hem to the cuff with the uneven backstitch.

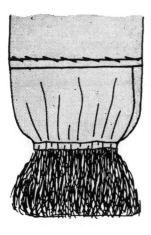

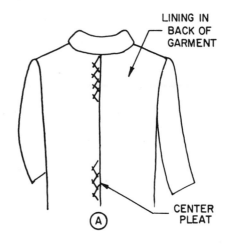

Figure 94

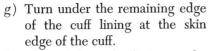

g) Turn under the remaining edge of the cuff lining at the skin edge of the cuff.

h) Pin and hem the lining to the fur cuff.

6. Construct and insert windbreakers in the sleeve.

a) Cut a piece of lining 6 in. wide and long enough to go around the lower sleeve plus seam allowance (Figure 93).

b) Stitch the two narrow edges together.

c) Press the seam open.

d) Turn under the upper and lower edges ⅝ in. and stitch ½ in. from the creased edge.

e) Insert ¼ in. wide elastic in one hem. Draw up the elastic to fit the wrist. Fasten the ends of the elastic to each other.

f) Turn the lined sleeve inside out.

g) Keep the raw edges of the hems on the outside and place it around the lower edge of the lined sleeve (Figure 94). The elastic edge of the storm sleeve should be placed on top of the bottom edge of the sleeve.

h) Sew the top of the windbreaker to the lining of the sleeve.

i) Turn the sleeve hair side out.

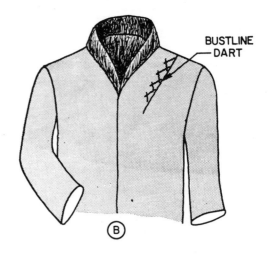

Figure 95

7. Fasten the darts and pleat. The darts and pleat are anchored into place with the catch stitch (Figure 95, A and B). The dart is sewn ⅔ of its length starting at the top. The center back pleat is fastened at the neck edge for 4 in. If the pleat is long, it should be fastened at the waistline for 1 in.

6

PROCEDURES FOR FUR ACCESSORIES

MINK BOA

A boa is a circle of fur which is worn around the neck. It may be a single or double circle of matching skins. Boas may be made from new or used skins.

If the boa is made of used skins, they must be disassembled. Cut the threads holding the outside edges of the rear legs together and cut across the base of the tail. Turn the skin inside out and remove the interfilling, skull, jaw, and eyes. We will deal with constructing a mink boa from new skins.

Procedure.

NOTE: See the chapters on marking, cutting, and sewing.

1. Turn the pelt skin side out.
2. Mark the cut-outs for the front legs and ears.
   a) The length of the leg opening is approximately 3 to 4 in. depending on the size of the mink skin (Figure 96).
   b) The length of the ear opening is approximately 1 in. (Figure 97).
3. Cut out the openings.
4. Sew the openings together.
   a) Begin to sew at the middle of the leg opening and sew toward either end.
   b) In the ear opening, the sewing begins at the right end and continues toward the left.
5. With a ball-point pen, mark the center of the belly of the mink skin. *Do not cut the grotzen line* (Figure 96).
6. Cut the mink skin on the center-marked line.
7. With a ball-point pen, make a 1 in. line on the back, beginning at the base and center of the tail (Figure 98).
8. Detach the tail and the hind legs from the body.

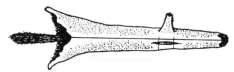

Figure 96

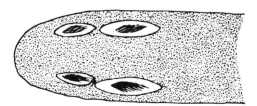

Figure 97

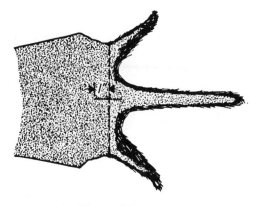

Figure 98

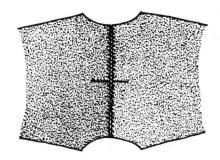

Figure 99

a) Mark the cutting line across the base of the tail and the top of the rear legs.

b) Cut the skin.

9. Repeat Steps 1 to 8 on all the skins to be used in the boa.

10. Match the center markings of the two mink skins.

11. Sew the two edges together starting at the center marking (Figure 99).

12. Dampen the skin side with a sponge and warm water.

13. Shape the mink skins over a boa board or specially shaped wires. (See p. 79 for a description of the board and wires.)

a) Place the center back seam on the center of the boa board (Figure 100, A).

b) Shape the flat skin to the boards (Figure 100, B).

c) Nail the skins to the boa board with push pins placed on the belly side. Begin nailing at the center seam and nail evenly on both sides (Figure 100, C).

d) Be sure that the grotzen line follows the center of the board.

e) Work out the excess fullness on the inside curve toward the cut edge (Figure 100, D).

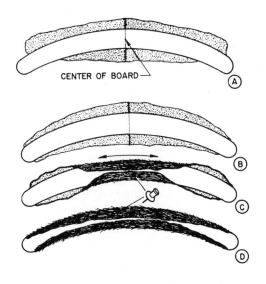

CENTER OF BOARD

Figure 100

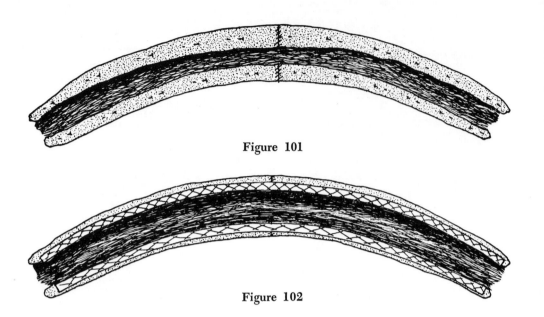

Figure 101

Figure 102

f) Allow the skins to dry thoroughly (approximately eight hours).

g) Remove the skins from the board.

14. Tape the cut edges along the length of the skins.

a) Turn the fur, skin side out, on the curved edges.

b) Pin the two layers of fur together (Figure 101).

c) Pin the seam tape to the cut edges.

i) Place the seam tape an equal distance from the top and bottom curved edges (Figure 102).

NOTE: The distance between the two rows of seam binding is the width of the velvet ribbon, usually 2 in. wide.

d) Sew the seam tape to the skin with a catch stitch. The pins are removed as the tape is sewn to the skin.

e) Trim off the excess skin. OPTIONAL: Cold tape may be used in place of seam tape, thus eliminating sewing.

15. Attach the velvet ribbon. Velvet ribbon is used to fill in the area between the two taped edges to make a tube in which an interfilling is placed. The width of the ribbon depends upon the size of the mink skins being used. The color of the ribbon should harmonize with the color of the fur. Two in. wide ribbon is the most common width. The length of the ribbon is the length of the two skins sewed together plus 6 in.

a) Make a gathering stitch, either by hand or machine, along one finished edge of the velvet ribbon. The stitched edge is the top edge of the ribbon.

b) Sew the bottom edge of the ribbon to the lower or longer curved taped skin edge. The ribbon is held with the pile side facing the hair side of the fur.

c) Sew from right to left beginning at the location of the closed ear opening. Use a whipping stitch.

i) Allow 3 in. of ribbon to extend beyond the closed ear areas on both skins.

ii) The ribbon and skins should be equal in length on either side of the center seam.

NOTE: One mink skin may be longer, but when sewing ribbon to the skins, make each side of the boa equal in length.

d) Fold the boa, skin side out, on the two curved sides, being careful not to distort the curves.

e) Pull the gathering thread on the top edge of the ribbon so that it will follow the curve of the upper taped fur edge. Work out as much fullness as possible. The larger the skins, the smaller the amount of fullness in the ribbon.

f) Pin the ribbon to the skin under it. OPTIONAL: Use 4 in. hair clips on the skin side of the curves to hold the upper or shorter curve in place.

g) Sew the ribbon to the top taped curved edge beginning at right hand end. Leave an 8 in. opening at the center of the boa.

16. Shape the ends.

a) Place the boa with the ribbon side up and the skin side down.

b) Fold the velvet ribbon ends back and sew the ribbon to the two taped skin edges. A pocket is formed by the fold of the ribbon (Figure 106). The pocket should be no deeper than 3 in.

c) Push pins through the skin at

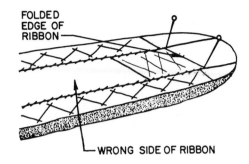

Figure 103

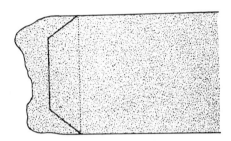

Figure 104

the end of the seam of the ribbon and the skin (Figure 103).

d) Turn the boa skin side up.

e) Draw a straight line between the two pin marks.

f) Measure ½ in. toward the center of the boa and draw a straight line parallel to the line made in *e* (Figure 104).

g) Draw diagonal lines between the ends of the lines made in *e* and *f*.

h) Cut the lines made in *f* and *g*.

i) Turn the boa ribbon side up.

j) Mark and cut the ribbon side of the boa to correspond with the diagonal of the previous cut made in *g*.

NOTE: If the skin were laid

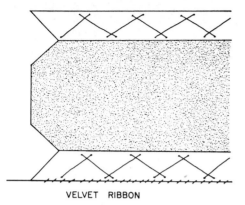

VELVET RIBBON

Figure 105

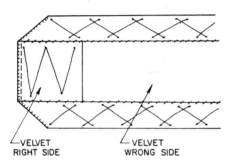

VELVET
RIGHT SIDE

VELVET
WRONG SIDE

Figure 106

flat, the ends of the boa would appear as shown in Figure 105.

17. Finish the ends. The ends of a boa are critical and care must be taken to give them a professional appearance. The tension of the sewing must be somewhat tight so that no skin shows through the hair. It may be necessary to put a second row of stitches over the first row. If the threads or skin still continue to show, place a row of small stitches under the whipping stitches and pull the thread slightly. These stitches are perpendicular to the whipping stitch.

   a) Sew the two diagonally cut edges together.

   b) Sew the folded edge of the ribbon to the straight edge of the skin (Figure 106).

18. Attach the interfilling. Use synthetic wadding or lamb's wool for the interfilling.

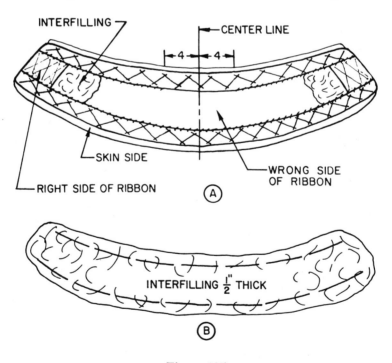

INTERFILLING

CENTER LINE

INTERFILLING

4   4

SKIN SIDE

WRONG SIDE
OF RIBBON

RIGHT SIDE OF RIBBON   Ⓐ

INTERFILLING $\frac{1}{2}$" THICK

Ⓑ

Figure 107

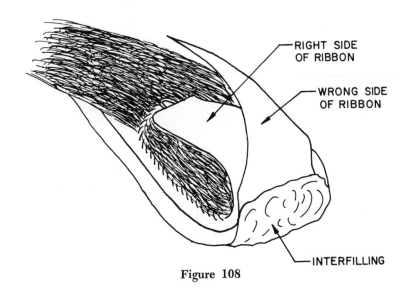

RIGHT SIDE OF RIBBON

WRONG SIDE OF RIBBON

INTERFILLING

Figure 108

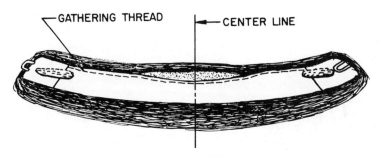

GATHERING THREAD

CENTER LINE

Figure 109

a) Fill the velvet ribbon pocket.

Push the interfilling toward the folded edge.

Feather the opposite end of the interfilling.

Sew the interfilling to the top layer of ribbon without the thread showing on the right side of the boa.

NOTE: Figure 107, A, shows the inside of the ribbon side of the boa.

b) Shape the interfilling to the boa.

Cut the synthetic interfilling ¾ in. larger than the width of the sewn pelts, measuring from the skin side.

Pull apart wool interfilling by feathering it so that it is twice the width of the skins.

c) Center the interfilling on the skin side of the top of the boa.

d) Sew the interfilling to the skin with uneven basting stitches near the top and bottom curved lengthwise edges (Figure 107, B). Keep the thread loose and the length of the stitch into the skin small.

19. Turn the boa to the hair side by pulling the ends through the center opening (Figure 108).

20. Fit the ribbon into the center opening and sew the ribbon to the hair side, using a hemming stitch. (NOTE: The ribbon is laid on top of hair side of the pelt. The two edges are *not* whipped together.) (Figure 109)

21. Remove the basting stitches from the ribbon.
22. Finish the boa.
    a) Sew a hook on the ribbon side of the right end at the center (Figure 110).
    b) Sew an eye on the ribbon side of the left end at the center.
    c) Cover both the eye and the hook with a small piece of matching ribbon, about 2 x 1½ in., placing the finished edges of the ribbon on the hook-and-eye end. Turn under the raw edges of the ribbon.
    d) Sew the ribbon with a blind stitch along the hook-and-eye end and along the two turned edges.

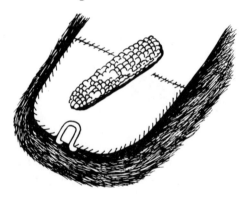

Figure 110

e) Insert the jaws. The location of the jaws depends upon the use of the boa. They may be inserted crosswise, lengthwise, or diagonally. The jaws are placed crosswise if the boa is to be worn on top of a collar such as a shawl collar. When the boa is to be worn in a circle, place the jaw straight on the left end and diagonally on the right.

Determine the location of the jaws.

Cut two layers of ribbon with a razor blade making the cut as small as possible.

Insert the long end of the jaw first and then bring the ribbon over the small end.

Sew the remaining end of the ribbon covering the hook, eye, and jaw as far as the ribbon of the boa.

f) Sew the initials onto the velvet ribbon.
23. Double Boas. A boa may have more than two full skins. In this case, the skins require skillful arrangement to produce an attractive neckpiece (Figure 111). If the skins are short, the tails may be used to give added length.

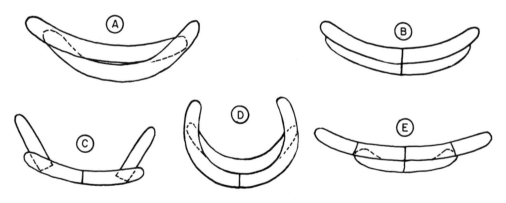

Figure 111

Figure 112

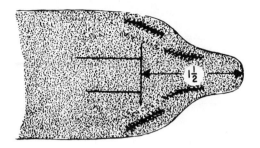

Figure 113

MINK NECK SCARF

Full skins are used to construct neck scarves. All parts of the original animal skin are used for mounting. Furriers refer to mounting as the process of using a tanned skin to prepare a lifelike form to be worn on the shoulders. The current trend is to eliminate the front legs in mink skins. If a part of the skin is missing or badly torn, it must be replaced with a matching part.

The number of skins used in a neck scarf will depend upon the size of the skins, the size of the wearer, and the amount of money to be invested in skins. The price of a male skin is approximately twice that of a female skin. Prices fluctuate with the current fashion trend. An important fact to remember when deciding upon a fur scarf is its proportion in relation to the individual. For example, too heavy a fur on a shorter-than-average woman will seem ostentatious. Buy quality rather than quantity.

Skins may be contoured to permit ease in wearing. A contoured neck scarf is made from two skins. Contoured skins will stay in place on the shoulders more readily than straight shaped skins. A contoured neck scarf is worn with the skins crosswise. The heads and tails of the skins are at either shoulder.

NOTE: If at any time work on a moist skin must be interrupted, put the skin in a plastic bag in a refrigerator. The fur will safely remain moist for a week. It is inadvisable to allow the skins to dry out and moisten them again.

Procedure.
Prepare the skin for nailing.

1. Follow Steps 1, 2, 3, and 4 in the section on boas, p. 116.
2. Sew together the eye openings. No skin should be showing from the hair side when the sewing is completed.
3. Shape the ears. The ears were cut out of the head because they were shriveled and lacked the semblance of ears. They must be soaked in warm water to make the ear tissue very soft and pliable. They then can be shaped into a half circle (Figure 112).
   a) Place the cut-out ears in warm water for fifteen to twenty minutes.
   b) Remove the ears from the water and shape them.
   c) Cut off the excess skin with a scissors.
   d) Fold the ear in half.
   e) Sew the straight edges of the ear together, starting at the folded edge.
4. Set the ears.
   a) Mark the new location for the ears.
      Measure 1½ in. back from the tip of the nose (Figure 113).

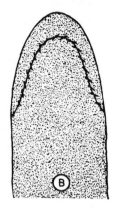

Figure 114

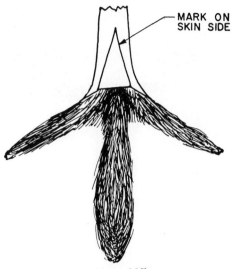

MARK ON SKIN SIDE

Figure 115

Draw a horizontal line across the head.

Place a thumb on the center of the head. Draw two parallel lines from the horizontal line back toward the tail. The lines should be longer than the length of the base of the sewed ear.

b) Cut the ear openings.

c) Insert an ear in either opening and sew it to the skin of the head, placing the folded edge toward the tail. After both ears are sewed, check the appearance from the hair side to see that they are identical. Occasionally one ear must be reset.

5. Sew together any small head cuts, tears, or hair breaks. Hair breaks often occur in tanning when the hair is accidentally removed from the skin. Cut out the skin area and sew the edges together. It is not necessary to close tattoo markings which may occur in the head area, unless the holes are very large.

6. Sew the mouth opening closed (Figure 114).

a) Place only the head in warm water for ten to fifteen minutes.

b) Cut off any excess skin which has been left around the mouth opening. At the ends of the opening, the skin is usually

thick. Cut off the thickened skin and skive the upper edge if it is very thick.

c) Pull up the skin on the underside of the head so that it meets the edge of the top side. The underside should have a smooth curved edge. If the edge is not even, cut it to resemble the original shape.

d) Sew the two edges of the mouth together beginning at the center and working toward either end. Shape the underside to fit the top edge.

Sew the edges firmly with a double thread using the whipping stitch and keep the stitches close together.

Turn the head, hair side out. If the thread shows, a row of perpendicular stitches is placed under the first row of whipping stitches. Stitches are placed on the skin side.

7. Reset the rear end of the belly side. Sometimes the belly side of the skin has a large V between the hind legs. This opening was made during the pelting or tanning.

a) Mark a larger V beginning at the base of the legs and con-

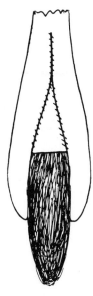

Figure 116

tinue to slightly above the original opening (Figure 115).

b) Cut out the V.

c) Drop the cut-out section so that the lower edge will correspond with the lower edge of the back.

d) Mark the placement of the cut-out with lines perpendicular to the cut edges.

e) Sew the opening closed beginning at the pointed end.

f) Sew the cut-out section into position sewing first along one side and then along the other side (Figure 116).

8. Turn the fur hair side out.

9. Insert the rubber skull. The nose of a mink should be long and sleek. In order to make a narrow pointed nose, it may be necessary to trim

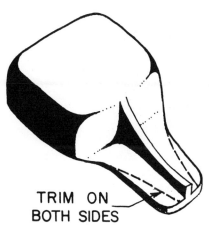

TRIM ON BOTH SIDES

Figure 117

the nose of the rubber skull so that it is less boxy and wide (Figure 117).

a) Slide the skull through the body to the closed end of the head.

b) Work the head skin over the rubber skull. Maneuver the excess skin toward the back of the skull.

Nail the whole skin.

1. Turn the fur with the skin side out.

2. Dampen the skin of the body, tail, and legs with a sponge and warm water. The skin should feel moist but not soaking wet.

3. Turn the fur so that the hair side is out.

4. Place the fur on straight or curved wires (Figure 118). The fur on the shaped wires is fastened to a flat nailing board.

Figure 118   NAILS

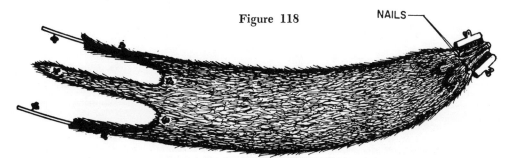

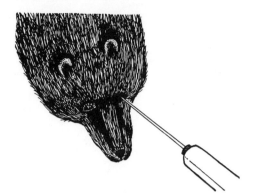

Figure 119

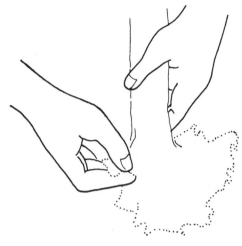

Figure 121

Figure 120

a) The rounded end of the wire must fit snugly at the base of the rubber skull.

b) The grotzen line must run down the exact middle of the form.

c) Wrap the rear legs around the wire and use push pins to hold them in place.

d) The length of the belly side must correspond with the length of the back. Pin the two open edges of the skin together with push pins.

e) Straighten out the tail and nail it on the nailing board skin side down.

5. Put one brad through the head to the nailing board at the location of either eye. This brad helps to hold the skin in place.

6. Place small pinch clips over the hair side of either side of the nose with one end of the clip fitting snugly into the eye area.

7. Shape the ears.
   a) Open the ears so that they look like a fan.
   b) See that both ears are identical.

8. Allow the fur to dry thoroughly for approximately eight to ten hours.

NOTE: When the shaped-wire form is used for nailing, it is placed on top of a wooden board. Push pins and brads are used to hold the wire and fur in the desired positions. When the wooden forms are used, the push pins and brads are put directly into the wood of the form.

Remove the fur from the shaped form.

Insert the glass eyes.

1. Use an ice pick or other pointed instrument to make a hole through the skin and skull at the location of the eyes (Figure 119).

2. Separate the two glass eyes by cutting the wire shank in half.

3. Insert the wire shank in the holes made into the head.

4. Turn the skin fur side out.

5. Fit the eyes tightly into the skull.

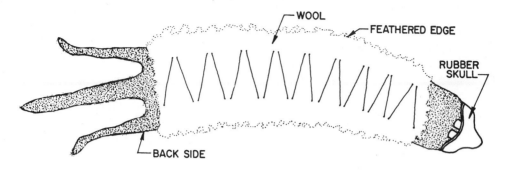

Figure 122

6. Twist the wires snugly together on the inside of the skull (Figure 120). Bend the long ends into the rubber skull.

Attach the interfilling.

1. Use lamb's wool or synthetic inter-filling.
   a) Use an amount of lamb's wool twice the width of the skin. Feather the edges of the wool (Figure 121); or
   b) Cut the synthetic interfilling slightly larger than the size of the skin.
2. Place a small quantity of inter-filling into the rubber skull.
3. Sew the interfilling to the skin side.
   a) Place the center of the wool on the grotzen (Figure 122).
   b) Sew the wool to the skin using a large size catch stitch; or
   c) Sew the synthetic interfilling to the belly side using two rows of uneven basting placed near the cut edges.

Turn the fur to the hair side.

Close the tail end opening.

1. Sew together the two edges of the tail starting at the tip. This sewing is done from the hair side. The guard hair may be moistened with wet finger tips to help keep it flat and out of the way.

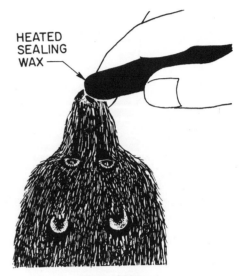

Figure 123

2. Sew the edges of the hind legs to-gether.
3. Sew the back and belly ends to-gether between the rear legs.
   NOTE: Sometimes it is necessary to slash the base of the tail on either side. This will help to give a smooth appearance on the back. This tail end of the mink should not look bubbly, gathered, or full.

Touch up the face.

1. Heat the tip of the sealing wax over direct heat.
2. Apply a small amount of wax directly to the nose of the mink skin (Figure 123).
3. Smooth the wax with your finger-tips.

PROCEDURES FOR FUR ACCESSORIES 127

4. Apply a small amount of clear shellac on the nose to flatten the hair. Move the fingers toward the eyes.

Assemble the finished skins for a contoured neck scarf.

1. Sew the head of one of the skins to the area just above the tail of the second skin.
2. Make three swing tacks approximately ¾ in. long. Place one swing tack near the tip of the nose and the other two at the outer edge of the skull approximately 1½ in. behind the single swing tack.
3. Insert the jaw in the skull by cutting from the hair side at the base of the rubber skull. Slide the long uncovered end of the jaw into the slit toward the nose end. Work the skin over the short end of the jaw. Keep the slit as short as possible. The long uncovered metal arm of the jaw should be inside the rubber skull.
4. Sew the crocheted ball snap to the belly side of the fur.
5. Attach the arm strap. Make a strap 1 by 8 in. from soft lining fabric. Turn the raw edges under and sew the strap to the belly side of the skins. Use the catch stitch. Sew the initials to the strap.

NOTE: Initials may be sewed directly to the skin if no strap is sewn to the skin.

Assemble the straight-shaped skins (Figure 124). There are many different ways of arranging three or more skins. The diagrams indicate different patterns.

1. In addition to sewing the head of one skin onto the body of a second skin, two skins may be attached to each other side by side. One-inch swing tacks are used to attach the two skins to each other when the skins are parallel. At least three 1 in. swing tacks are used to attach two skins together when they are parallel. More swing tacks may be used when using large size skins.
2. It is interesting to note that a neck scarf can be made longer or shorter by the pattern used to arrange the skins.

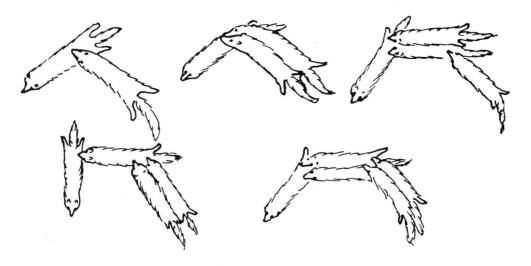

Figure 124

COLLARS

Fur trim adds a touch of elegance to a suit, dress, or coat. It is important that it fit perfectly; therefore, a pattern must be made of the area on which the trim will be placed.

Fur collars are usually made so that the hair does not touch the skin of the neck. The fur extends downward from the break line of the collar, covering the fall. The fur collar may extend beyond the outer edge of the garment collar. The outer edge of the fur collar may have an entirely different shape from the garment collar, but the inside edge must correspond exactly to the shape of the break line of the garment.

Establishing the Pattern for a Collar.

1. Put the garment on the individual and close all the fastenings.
2. Work with only one half of the garment, unless the collar is not symmetrical.
3. Mark the break line of the garment collar with straight pins, pushing them through the fabric. If the garment has a lapel, extend the pins along the break line of the lapel. Place the pins about 1 in. apart (Figure 125).
4. Remove the garment.
5. Place the underside of the garment collar on top of a piece of brown paper.
6. Allow the garment collar to assume its natural shape.
7. Push the pins which were placed on the break line of the garment collar through the brown paper (Figure 126). The pin holes in the paper will serve as a guide in Step 10 (Figure 127).
8. Using a ball-point pen on the brown paper, mark the garment collar at the center back, the front end, and the outer edge.

Figure 125

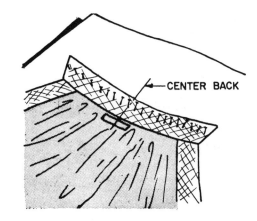

CENTER BACK

Figure 126

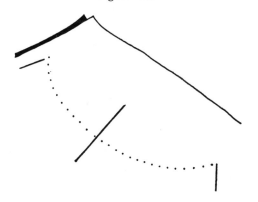

Figure 127

9. Remove the garment from the brown paper.
10. Draw a connecting line between the pin holes in the brown paper. This line represents the inner edge of the collar.

11. Draw a line ⅜ to ½ in. beyond the outer edge and center front of the collar (Figure 128). Do not add anything extra at the center back. The fur collar must be larger than the garment collar.

NOTE: If there is sufficient fur, the outside line may be greater than ½ in., and it does not have to follow the line of the garment collar. A shawl collar pattern may be designed with a notch to give the appearance of a convertible collar.

12. Cut out the paper pattern and try it on the garment collar. Check the top curve of the pattern with the break line of the garment collar. If the pattern covers the garment collar with sufficient ease, the fur collar will not look tight when completed.

13. The end of a shawl collar pattern should be 1 in. wide. Do not allow the fur collar pattern to be pointed at the ends.

Establishing the Pattern for a Fashion Detail.

Fur may be used for a fashion detail such as trim on a pocket, lower edge of a jacket or coat, cuff of a sleeve, front for a fabric handbag, and the crown of a hat.

To use fur for a fashion detail, a paper pattern must be made.

1. Pins are pushed through the fabric into brown paper in the line of the desired curve or outline.

2. The pin holes on the brown paper are connected with a straight or curved line.

3. Approximately ⅜ to ½ in. is added to the outside of the pattern. When the pattern is completed, it is placed on the skin side of the fur, marked, and cut out.

4. The outer edges of the fashion detail are reinforced, the edges taped, and the detail lined. See Steps 14 and 15 on pp. 131–132.

A pattern is made when covering a hat.

1. Pins are pushed through the top and bottom edges of the crown into brown paper. The resulting pattern will have a definite curve.

2. Before cutting the fur, check the pattern on either the hat frame or the hat. It should be slightly larger than the frame because the fur will be taken up somewhat as it is sewn.

3. If the fur is slightly large after reinforcing the edges, it can be held in when sewn to the hat frame.

Fur Collars from Whole Skins.

Fur collars may be made from the whole skin of mink, rabbit, fox, fitch, marten, and other animals. Although the following directions are written with mink fur in mind, they are applicable to fur from other small animals. When using fur from leopard, pony, mouton, muskrat, otter, Persian lamb, and pieced mink, follow the directions on p. 133.

Procedure.

1. Follow Steps 1, 2, 3, 4 as shown on page 116.

2. If *two* mink skins are used for the collar follow Steps, 5, 6, and 7, on p. 116.

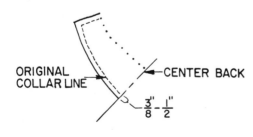

ORIGINAL COLLAR LINE ← CENTER BACK

$\frac{3}{8}$ - $\frac{1}{2}$"

Figure 128

3. Cut off the tail of the mink skin at the base of the tail (Figure 98, p. 117).
4. Mark the center of the belly and the back when using one skin.
5. Cut the skin on the marked lines.
6. Draw two sets of collar patterns. Cut out one set.
7. Place the brown paper with the uncut pattern on top of the nailing board.
8. Dampen the skin side of the mink with warm water and a sponge.
9. Nail out the mink. Generally the direction of the guard hair is toward the back; however, it may go toward the front depending upon the fashion.
   a) Place the grotzen edge of the mink skin toward the outer edge of the pattern.
   b) Place the tail end of the mink skin toward the center back.
   c) Shape each half of the mink skin to the pattern on the brown paper.
      Use push pins along the outer edge of the skin to pin baste it to the shape of the pattern. The skin will extend beyond the pattern.
      Work out the extra fullness toward the top and bottom edges and staple the skin to the nailing board with tote-size staples.
      Check the nailed out collar with the cut-out collar pattern to be sure that it has the proper neck edge curve and is large enough. (When the nailing is completed, the pattern on the brown paper is covered. Therefore, use the cut-out pattern to check the shape of the skin before it dries.)
      Allow the fur to dry thoroughly, approximately four to eight hours.
10. Remove the brown paper with the attached mink skin from the nailing board, leaving the staples in the fur.
11. Remove the staples from the mink skin.
12. Square the collar.
    a) Place the cut-out paper pattern on top of the nailed out skin (Figure 129).
    b) Mark the outer edges of the pattern on the skin.
    c) Cut the skin.
13. Apply dye to the edges from the skin side. This process is known as "tipping." When using dark-colored mink, tipping will prevent the light skin color from showing through the underfur (see Figure 59).
14. Sew the seam tape flat around the outer edges of the collar on the skin side using a catch stitch or a running catch stitch. The tape acts as a stay to prevent stretching (Figure 130). OPTIONAL: Cold tape may be used in place of steam tape. No sewing is required.
15. Sew a second seam tape around the outer edge of the collar using

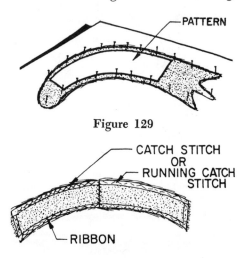

Figure 129

Figure 130

the whipping stitch. This tape is placed on the fur side.

NOTE: This tape should begin within the upper or lower back curve, not at the corner or ends of the collar.

16. Interfill the collar.

   a) The amount of interfilling will depend upon the effect desired. The more interfilling used, the fuller the collar will appear; however, it must not make the collar stiff.

   b) Use lamb's wool, boa stuffing, or several thicknesses of wool fabric.

   c) Fasten the interfilling to the skin side with loose, uneven basting stitches so that the thread does not show from the hair side.

17. Fold the second tape over onto the interfilling and fasten with uneven basting stitches keeping the outer edges smooth and symmetrical (Figure 131). It may be necessary to slash the tape on the upper edge and to pleat the tape at the corners and along the lower edge of the collar.

18. Apply the fastenings.

   a) Stud pins. Stud pins are used to make a collar detachable. The number of them will depend upon the size of the collar. Usually four pins are used. Two pins are placed near the front ends of the collar and two pins are located an equal distance from the center back. The shank end of the pin is sewn to the interfilling. The lining covers the base of the pin.

   b) Hooks and eyes. Hooks and eyes are placed at the front edge of the collar if it is so designed to fasten together. The choice of using either crocheted or uncovered hooks and eyes is dependent upon the size of the collar. Large collars require the crocheted fastener which is larger than the uncovered fastener.

   c) Snaps. When snaps are used, it is desirable to use covered snaps which will harmonize with the hair color of the fur. Snaps are sewn to the collar after the lining has been attached. The socket of the snap is sewn on the left side directly on top of the hair, and the ball of the snap is sewn to the lining on the right side of the collar.

   d) Buttonholes.

   Follow the steps on p. 108.

   Pull the second tape through the opening to the skin side.

   Sew the tape to the skin using a small uneven basting stitch.

   Indicate the length of the buttonhole by pushing pins through the lining at either end.

   Cut the lining between the pin markers.

   Turn under the raw edges of the lining and attach it with an uneven backstitch.

19. Line the collar.

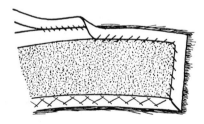

Figure 131

a) The fur collar may or may not be lined. If the fur collar is placed over a garment collar which has both a top and under collar, it may not be necessary to line the fur collar. When the fur collar is larger than the garment collar, it is necessary to line the fur collar. When lining a collar, use a *soft* fabric.

b) Cut the lining 1 in. larger than the size of the fur pattern on all sides. The lining may or or may not have a center seam. No underlining is necessary.

c) Place the lining section on top of the interfilling which is optional in some furs (Figure 132).

d) Turn under the lining edge and pin it to the tape. The lining should cover the tape. If necessary, trim the lining fabric so it is not bulky.

e) Attach the lining using an uneven backstitch. Keep the stitches invisible.

20. Attach the fur collar to the garment.

a) If stud pins are used, push the shank end of the stud pin through the garment collar and attach the catch end.

b) When a fur collar is attached permanently to a garment, the sewing is done between the front ends and along the upper edge of the collar. The

Figure 132

stitches must be kept hidden. When the collar is lined, it is not necessary to fasten it along the outer edge. When the fur collar is not lined, fasten it to the garment collar around the outer edge.

Collars from Assembled Fur.

Assembled fur consists of many small pieces of fur which are sewn together to give a large workable piece. This technique is found in plates of mink heads, tails, gills, narrows, ovals and paws. Muskrat backs and bellies, Persian lamb backs, Persian lamb paws, marmot backs, squirrel backs and sides, and many other furs which have been sewn together to form an area are included in this category.

The following procedure is followed when using mouton, leopard, otter, and pony.

1. It is important to determine the direction of the guard hair. Fashion and the amount of fur available will help to determine this direction. It may flow from the center back toward the front; toward the center back, or outward from the neckline. If the fur has a stripe, either simulated or natural, this feature must be taken into consideration too.

2. When a collar is completed, the direction of the guard hair or any stripe must give a continuous effect. The stripe or direction of the guard hair should not "run off" the collar. When using Persian lamb, little or no consideration has to be given to the direction of the curl. To achieve a continuous line, the collar pattern is slashed at various intervals. See directions on p. 134.

Assembled Fur With the Stripe or Direction of the Guard Hair Following the Outer Edge of the Collar.

Procedure.

1. Follow the directions on p. 129 to establish a pattern for the collar.
2. Mark the location of the stripe or direction of the guard hair.
   a) From the hair side push pins through the skin on a stripe or on the straight direction of the guard hair.
   b) Turn the fur to the skin side.
   c) Mark the location of the pins with a straight line using a ball-point pen.
3. Slash the collar pattern at several intervals from the neck edge outward so that the outer edge of the collar forms a straight line (Figure 51, A and B).
4. Lay the outside edge of the slashed collar pattern on the straight line made in Step 2, a.
5. Pin the pattern in position.
6. Mark the pattern on the skin side with a ball-point pen.
7. Cut out the collar sections.
8. Sew together the collar sections using the whipping stitch (see p. 89).
9. Flatten all of the seams (see p. 89).
10. Nail out the collar.
    a) Place the collar, skin side up, on a nailing board.
    b) Using a sponge, apply warm water to the skin side.
    c) Fasten the collar to the nailing board with push pins or staples.
    d) Allow the collar to dry four to eight hours.
    e) Square the collar by placing the original collar pattern on the skin side (Figure 129).
    Using the original pattern, mark the outer edges of it on the skin.
    Cut off any irregularities of shape.
    f) Check the new fur collar on the garment to be sure it has the proper size and shape.
11. Proceed with Steps 14–20.

Assembled Fur With the Stripe or Direction of the Guard Hair Radiating Out From the Neckline.

Procedure.

1. Draw a straight line perpendicular to the stripe of direction of the guard hair on the skin side.
2. Follow Step 3, above.
3. Lay the outside edge of the slashed collar pattern on the straight line. It may be necessary to use several pieces of fur rather than one continuous strip. The outside edge of the collar is placed on a line which is perpendicular to the stripe and/or direction of the guard hair.
4. Follow Steps 5–11, above.

Wedding Ring Collar

The wedding ring fur collar is a circle of fur which starts at the neck edge or slightly below in the front and drops to 1 to 3 inches below the neck edge at the center back.

When there is no pattern for this style of collar, one is made by cutting and darting brown paper until the desired shape is obtained. After it is made, the fur is nailed (see p. 131). To finish the collar see pp. 131–132.

A cardigan neckline garment is the basis for the wedding ring collar. In a fur garment the neck edge is finished with either grosgrain ribbon or a fur facing.

There are two basic shapes for this type of collar. The first collar is only slightly shaped. Use a slant hemming stitch to attach the lower edge of the fur collar to the garment. Crocheted hooks and eyes are used at the front edges to fasten the collar together.

The second shape is similar to that of a convertible collar which is sewn at the neck edge. Instead of sewing the collar to the neck edge, place it 1 to 3 inches below the neck edge at the center back. It begins at the neck edge in the front. The location of the center back of the collar depends on the depth of the stand. The wider the stand, the lower the collar is placed at the center back. The collar is attached to the garment at the lower edge of the stand with a slant hemming stitch.

Two furs may be used in this collar. The stand is the same fur as the body of the garment; the fall can be contrasting. When a contrasting fur is used, the dividing line is a break line. If this style of collar is used on a leather garment, the stand can be fabric or leather with the fur beginning at the break line. Crocheted hooks and eyes are used to fasten the collar together at the center front.

FUR LININGS

Fur used for a lining will give extra warmth to a cloth or leather coat. If the lining is detachable, the coat will be more versatile because of a longer wearing season. Fur lining need not be as high a quality as is necessary for a fur garment.

The same general techniques used to construct a fur garment are applicable. Usually only the shell of the garment is lined. Sleeve lining is made of fabric and attached to the fur lining.

Procedure.
Use the pattern for the lining of the garment.

Remove the ⅝ in. seam allowance on the pattern tissue.

Lay the pattern on the skin side after the fur has been nailed (see p. 83).

Mark the pattern on the skin side (see p. 85).

Cut the pattern pieces from the fur (see p. 92).

Tape all the edges (see p. 100).
Sew together the darts and the underarm and shoulder seams.

Sew ⅝ in. grosgrain ribbon around the outer edge and armscye of the lining (see p. 110).

Turn *only* the ribbon to the skin side and sew it to the tape (see p. 110).

Attach the ball side of the snap tape on top of the grosgrain ribbon around the outside edge, except the bottom edge. Snap tape comes in various colors. The tape color should be inconspicuous. If only light-colored tape is available, dye it to match the garment.

The socket side of the snap tape is sewn into place on the front facing of the garment.

7

WHAT ABOUT MINK?

A new sewing adventure awaits the home sewer when she sews with mink. She may use one small skin to make a simple round collar or a pair of cuffs; however, several skins may be used to make a neck scarf or a double boa.

Select the best quality mink skin within the desired price range. Consideration must also be given to the color, which should be complimentary to the wearer and the garment on which it will be worn.

It is interesting to note that mink always has two color names. One color name is used by the mink rancher and the other by the marketing association through which the rancher sells his skins.

Before World War I wild mink represented a very high percentage of the pelts marketed. Then in the 1920's a boom in mink ranching took place. Ranch mink is chocolate brown. Occasionally mink of unusual colors occurs. These are called mutations.

The first mutation to demand much attention was platinum, a brownish gray color. It was found at two Wisconsin ranches as early as 1931. Seven Wisconsin ranchers interested in furthering the development of platinum mink contributed enough skins to make a full-length let-out mink coat. This coat was sold at a benefit auction on New Year's Eve, 1942. The price received was $17,000.

The second mutation developed was pastel, which was in evidence in the mid-1940's. Since then colors ranging from pure white to very dark black have been produced.

Most mink ranchers, whether large or small, belong to a marketing organization. Mink skins are sold at auctions in New York, Milwaukee, Minneapolis, and Seattle.

Marketing organizations include GLMA, AMRA, EMBA, and several smaller groups.

GLMA signifies the Great Lakes Mink Association and is associated with breeders of both dark and mutant mink. Formerly this organization dealt only with dark-colored pelts.

AMRA, the American Mink Ranchers' Association, is based in Milwaukee, Wisconsin. It handles both dark and mutation mink, with trademark names for the mutation colors.

EMBA is a coined word representing Mutation Mink Breeders Association. To this association belong only ranchers who breed mutation colors. They market mink in fourteen color groupings and two qualities. The "Rare Quality" is an elite collection of the very top pelts of each year's crop and are specially stamped. This quality uses the following trademarks:

Aeolian, natural taupe
Arcturus, natural lavender beige
Argenta, natural gray
Autumn Haze, natural brown
Azurene, natural blue-gray
Cerulean, natural blue
Desert Gold, natural light brown
Diadem, natural pale brown
Jasmine, pure white
Lilana, natural pale purple
Lunarine, natural demi-buff
Lutetia, natural gunmetal
Morning Light, natural blue beige
Rovalia, natural pink
Tourmaline, natural pale beige

"Royal Quality" is stamped on graded and selected pelts which must meet EMBA's standards, but are not quite up to those standards required for the "Rare Quality."

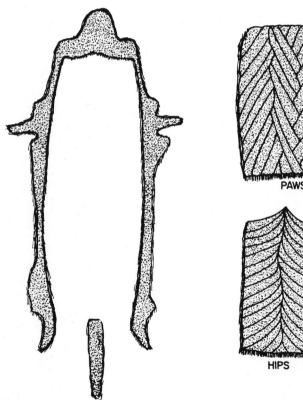

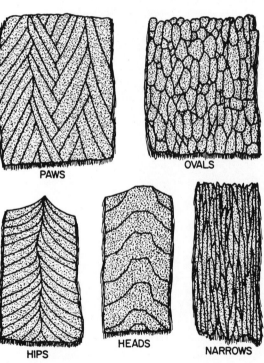

PAWS

OVALS

HIPS

HEADS

NARROWS

Figure 133

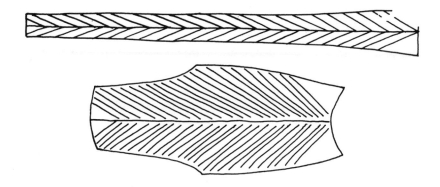

Figure 134

Because of the very excellent wearing quality of mink, every section of the pelt is used in garment making. After the back is removed from a pelt, the scraps are collected and sent to Kastoria, Greece. Here these scraps are graded, sorted, and sewed into lengths of matched fur. These lengths are called plates. From these plates garments are constructed. Plates are made entirely of gills, heads, tails, narrows, ovals, and paws (Figure 133). Each of these plates has a distinct sewing pattern.

Letting-out is a procedure of lengthening a pelt by cutting and sewing the sections together (Figure 134). A pelt is first cut into two equal halves along the grotzen and belly. Each half is cut into many diagonal sections. They are sewed together again after dropping each one $\frac{3}{16}$ to $\frac{3}{8}$ in. The two halves are sewed together along the grotzen line. After the skin is completely sewed together, it can be two or three times its original length, but one third to one fourth its original width.

Split skin refers to joined halves which have been split on the grotzen and belly (Figure 135). The pelt is first cut into equal halves. The grotzen edge is sewed to the belly edge of the adjacent pelt.

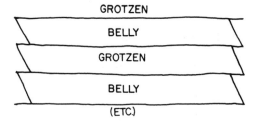

Figure 135

8

CARE
OF
FUR

The care of fur is both easy and inexpensive. The life of fur can be lengthened or shortened depending upon the care given to it.

Fur should be cleaned periodically by a professional fur cleaner. Since special cleaning equipment in the form of huge revolving drums is necessary, it is inadvisable to try cleaning fur at home.

Store all furs in paper or cloth garment bags—*never in plastic bags*. Furs need freely circulating air to prevent the skin from drying and the hair from being crushed and broken off.

Hang furs on wide hangers, preferably padded. Never allow a fur garment to hang on a wire hanger. Stoles may be hung crosswise on specially designed hangers. The center back of the stole should lie across the horizontal arm of the hanger.

To help eliminate excessive drying of the skin, keep furs at home in the coolest closet. In off seasons, the garment should be stored in vaults where the temperature and humidity are kept constant.

Avoid subjecting fur to friction. Constant carrying of a purse, books, or packages under the arm or the use of a shoulder strap will wear it down. Automobile seat covers will break off the guard hairs. When sitting, open the bottom button or hook. Pockets will show less signs of wear if they are not used. An inside pocket can be used instead. Fur styles with buttonholes should be avoided. Buttons may be sewn on the top of the right front for appearance, if desired.

A worn-looking fur garment can be restored to its original beauty by redesigning it to the current season's style. Keeping furs in style will protect your investment for a long time.

Rain and snow will not hurt a fur garment. However, a wet garment should be hung on a broad hanger away from direct heat. Allow the garment to dry untouched by other objects. When the garment is thoroughly dry, shake it firmly.

A few more "don'ts":

1. Don't pin flowers or corsages to fur.
2. Don't apply perfume directly to fur —the alcohol in perfume dries out the skin and stiffens the guard hairs.
3. Don't mothproof furs with chemical sprays.
4. Don't wear heavy jewelry where it will rub against the fur.

The Federal Fur Products Law

The owner of a fur garment wants to know how to protect her investment. She will be interested to know that the government took steps to safeguard her purchase before she made it.

The fur masquerade is over due to the passage of the Federal Fur Products Labeling Act on August 9, 1952. This act established a rigid code for presenting information about furs. Every fur selling for more than twenty dollars must have the following information on the invoice, the label, and in advertising:

1. Name: The animal's true English name, printed no smaller than 12 point, or pica-size type.
2. Origin: The name of the country of origin must be given for all imported furs.
3. Treated: If the fur has been bleached, dyed, tip-dyed or pointed, it must be indicated.
4. Pieced: If the garment is entirely or partially made up of paws, bellies, sides, flanks, or gills, this fact must be disclosed.
5. Used or secondhand: Furs must be identified as such in each case.

The size of the tag carrying the required information must be no smaller than 1¾ x 2¾ in.

GLOSSARY OF FUR TERMS

AMRA. A Milwaukee marketing association handling dark and mutation mink.

Assembled fur. A workable piece of fur which contains many small pieces of fur sewn together.

Bend-back taping. The turning of the second tape, which is sewn to the outer edges, and fastened to the skin side of the fur with an uneven basting stitch.

Boa. A circle of fur worn around the neck.

Breath of Spring. A paler shade of a designated color when referring to mink fur colors.

Canvas. A temporary muslin garment made from the pattern. It is used to check the fit of the pattern. Alterations are made in this garment first and then transferred to the paper pattern before cutting the fur.

Curly-haired fur. Fur which has naturally curly hair. The curls go in many directions.

Dyeing. The process of applying dyestuffs to the hair either by immersion in a dye bath or by application with brush, feather, or spray in order to change the color of the hair or to accentuate its natural color.

EMBA. A coined word used by the Mutation Mink Breeders Association to identify their particular pelts. The association is a marketing organization serving 5,000 mink ranchers in the U. S.

Glazing. A method of giving luster to new and used furs.

GLMA. Great Lakes Mink Association. A marketing organization through which mink ranchers sell only dark-colored skins.

Grotzen. The center back of a pelt. Usually the hair over this area is darker in color.

Guard hair. Long lustrous top covering of hair which protects the underfur.

Letting-out. The process of lengthening a pelt through a series of cuts and sewing the cut sections back together.

Long-haired fur. Furs which have a long guard hair and usually long underfur.

Mutation. Ranch-raised animals which are not the standard brown. Furs of special colors produced genetically by selective breeding under controlled conditions. Mink, fox, and nutria are produced in mutation colors.

Nailing. A process in which moisture is applied to the skin side and the fur is temporarily attached to a wooden surface with nails, push pins, or staples. Shapes may be eliminated, restored, or obtained in this process.

Natural. The color of the hair which has been produced by nature.

Oxidation. The action of air on the hair of fur which causes it to change color; light-colored hair turns darker and dark-colored hair turns lighter. The color change is gradual, but not always uniform. It occurs in both natural and dyed furs.

Plates. A commercial unit of assembled fur measuring 18 x 48 in.

Reinforcing. Adding strength to the skin side by applying tape, stay cloth, or chemicals.

Replacement. The addition of fur to adjust or fill in a given area.

Scarf. A neckpiece made from one or more full skins.

Shearing. Cutting the hair to even or shorten it in depth.

Shell. The garment unit which contains the back and front.

Short-haired fur. Fur having short guard hair and short underfur.

Skin-on-skin. A method of sewing pelts together without changing the length or width. The head of one pelt is attached to the tail end of the adjacent pelt.

Squaring. Cutting the nailed fur garment exactly to the pattern.

Staying. Reinforcing the fur on the skin side with fabric or a chemical.

Stewart. A lighter shade of a basic mutation color in mink.

Sweep. The bottom edge of a fur garment.

Taping. Applying tape to the skin side to reinforce edges or to stay large areas.

Tipping. The application of dye to the skin

side so that it will be the same shade as the underfur.

Underfur. The layer of comparatively short thick hair next to the skin.

Wild fur. Fur from trapped undomesticated animals rather than animals raised on ranches.

BOOKS

Ashbrook, Frank G. *Furs Glamorous and Practical.* New York: D. Van Nostrand Co., Inc., 1954.

Kaplan, David G. *The Fur Book.* New York: The Reuben H. Donnelley Corp., 1950.

Raphael, Samuel. *Advanced Fur Craftsmanship.* New York: Fur Craftsmanship Publishers, Inc., 1948.

Schwebke, Phyllis W. *How to Tailor.* Milwaukee: The Bruce Publishing Co., 1965.

BULLETINS

Butt, Gladys L. *Make Your Furs Wear Longer.* Ithaca, New York: Cornell Extension Bulletin 838, 1955.

All About Mink. Racine, Wis.: EMBA Mink Breeders Association.

EMBA Facts, the Magic of Mink. Racine, Wis.: EMBA Mink Breeders Association.

Facts You Should Know About Furs. Better Business Bureau.

Federal Trade Commission Rules and Regulations Under the Fur Products Labeling Act. Washington, D. C.: U. S. Government Printing Office.

How to Remodel and Repair Furs at Home. Woman's Day, Inc., 1957.

Treu, Ahbe Jay. *How to Remodel and Repair Furs for Pleasure or Profit.* Hicksville, New York: Fur Service.

Working With Fur. Good Housekeeping Bulletin 744.

SOURCES OF FUR

Tannery

National Superior Fur Dressing and Dyeing Company

4447–61 West Cortland Street
Chicago, Illinois 60639

Fur Supply Houses

The Singer Fur Company
190 North State Street
Chicago, Illinois 60601

Jos. Arenson & Sons
612 North Broadway Street
Milwaukee, Wisconsin 53211

Pollack's Furriers Supply Corp.
160 West 29th Street
New York, New York 10001

Rubenstein & Ziff
25 North 4th Street
Minneapolis, Minnesota 55401

Banasch's
125 West 5th Street
Cincinnati, Ohio 45202

Boa Boards

T. J. & P. Company
1501 Stemp Terrace
Madison, Wisconsin 53711

Interfilling, boa, 120-121; detachable collars, 132; mink neck scarf, 127; shaping, 121; types of, 120; use of, 80

Jaws, boa, 122; mink, 128
Jaw snaps, description of, 80

Leather softener, use of, 80, 83-84
Letting-out, 139; definition of, 142
Lining, back, 113; cuffs, 114-115; cutting, 111-112; darts, 112; detachable collar, 132-133; front, 113-114; lower edge, 114; removal of, 90; selection of, 80, 111; sewing to piping, 111; sewing darts and pleats in, 115; sewing to underlining, 112; sleeve, 112-113; storm sleeve, 115; uneven back stitch, 114

Marking, buttonholes, 108; cut edges, 85-86; direction of guard hair, 134; ends of boa, 119; garment break line, 129; guides for seams, 86, 102; location of stripe, 134; mink for boa, 116-117; mink resetting belly, 124-125; opening for hooks and eyes, 106-107; opening for pockets, 104; pattern for cutting, 85; pattern for used fur, 93-95; plain fur, 85; procedure, 85-86; replacement, 85; skins, collars, 130-131; striped fur, 85; worn areas, 85-91, 97-98
Mink, 136-139; arm strap, 128; assembling finished skins, 128; ball snaps, 128; closing tail, 127; ears, 123-124, 126; EMBA trademark, 138; glass eyes, 126-127; hair breaks, 124; interfilling neck scarf, 127; jaw, 128; letting-out, 139; marketing organizations, 136-138; moistening, 123; mutation, 71, 136; pieced, 139; plates, 139; price, 123; rare quality, 138; regal quality, 138; skin arrangement, 128; split skin, 139; swing tack, 128; tipping, 99; touching up face of, 127-128
Muslin, 80-81
Mutation, definition of, 142

Nailing, collar, 92; collar, mink skins, 131; collar, striped or straight hair, 134; definition of, 142; garment shell, 92; general techniques, 83-84; replacement area, 98; shaped boards, 79; shaped wires, 79; shaping mink ears, 123; sleeves, 92; solution used, 83; use of push pins in replacing, 98; whole mink skins for scarf, 125-126
Nailing board, description of, 76; use of in nailing replacement, 98; use of, 83-84
Natural, definition of, 142

Neck scarf, assembling finished skins, 128; mink, 123-128
Needles, 77; glover's, 77

Opening, mink, sewing leg and ear, 116; original garment, 90; used skins, 116
Oxidation, definition of, 142; dyeing and, 98

Paper collar pattern, 129-130; fashion detail pattern, 130; use of, 81
Patching. *See* Replacing
Pattern, alteration of, 74; alteration of for button and buttonholes, 74; alteration of for center back seam, 74; alteration of for collar, 95, 134; alteration of for patch pockets, 74; alteration of for raglan sleeve, 74; alteration of for stole, 97; button, 109; check points for fit, 75; detachable collar, 129-130; fashion detail, 130; fur lining, 135; hat, 130; marking on used fur, 93-94; muslin, 74, 80-81; selection of, 73-74; squaring collar, 131; use of dressmaker patterns, 74; wedding ring collar, 134-135
Pellon, 81
Pinch clip, use of, 77, 126
Pins, glass-head, 76
Piping, 110-111
Plates, definition of, 142; mink, 139
Pleat, sewing, 115
Pliers, use of, 77, 84
Pocket, 104-106; marking worn area of, 91; openings, 91, 104; pouch, 104-106; removal of, 90
Push pins, description of, 77; mink neck skins, nailing, 126; use in nailing, 83; use in nailing replacements, 98

Razor blade, 76, 82-83
Reinforcing, 100-102; definition of, 142; staying, 101-102; taping, 100-101
Replacement, definition of, 142
Replacing techniques, 97-98; shapes for, 97-98
Resetting belly side, 124-125
Rings, crocheted, use of, 79; closure, 108
Rubber gloves, 77
Ruler, 77
Running catch stitch, 87

Scarf, definition of, 142
Sealing wax, 81, 127
Seam binding, use of, 81
Seams, flattening, 79, 89, 102; sewing of, 89
Seam tape, attaching with catch stitch, 86; attaching with running catch stitch, 87; use in boa, 118; use in closures, 107; use